Automotive Custom Interiors

Photo courtesy of Mazda

Sue Elliot

motorbooks

First published in 2009 by MBI Publishing Company and Motorbooks,
an imprint of MBI Publishing Company, 400 First Avenue North, Suite 300,
Minneapolis, MN 55401 USA

Motorbooks titles are also available at discounts in bulk quantity for industrial
or sales-promotional use. For details write to Special Sales Manager at
MBI Publishing Company, 400 First Avenue North, Suite 300, Minneapolis,
MN 55401 USA.

To find out more about our books, visit us online at www.motorbooks.com.

ISBN-13: 978-0-7603-3288-7

Editor: Peter Schletty
Designer: Diana Boger

Printed in Singapore

Contents

Introduction

Texture abounds inside POSIES' art deco 1937 *Extremeliner*, which is loosely based on a combination of a 1937 Ford and the 1938 Hispano-Suiza H6C Saoutchik Xenia Coupe. The car's unique steering wheel matches its custom front wheels, and the speakers for its sound system hide behind wicker grilles. *Photo courtesy of POSIES*

Idea books are not exactly new. Kitchen and bath idea books have been around for years. In fact, the home and garden world is full of idea books.

But the automotive world is a different story. A custom automotive interior idea book *is* a new concept, and I sincerely hope this book will inspire you—maybe even make you laugh, or prompt you to call a friend to come over and take a look.

The whole idea is to get you thinking—and not just about things you can do to your hot rod, but also about things you can do to your kid's first car or to your daily driver or to the car you've always wanted to build for a long-haul road trip.

You know, one of the most beautiful things about the world of custom cars is its sheer diversity. People customize everything: vintage Plymouths, late-model Mercedes-Benzs, Hondas, Oldsmobiles, Studebakers, Mazdas, Minis, all manner of Fords and Chevrolets—from every decade, typically starting with the 1920s and reaching right up to the present. You'll find custom pickup trucks, SUVs, sedans, coupes, roadsters, even a few phantom body styles that never actually left an automaker's assembly line. Of course, some custom cars and trucks are incredibly high-buck buildups. Some are garage-built. And most run the gamut in between.

Sure, you can chop the top, shave the door handles, French the taillights. You can do a lot to the body of a vehicle. But when you look inside these custom cars and trucks, you'll find more variety in the interior than anyplace else. Oh, the inside. It's where people—and vehicles—really express their personalities. It's where you can spot people's quirks, their sense of humor, their desire for

The dark-over-light dash treatment with ambient lighting wraps beautifully into the doors of the Buick Riviera concept. And the gorgeous, cascading console is covered in suede-like Alcantara. The controls on the center of the dash include a touch screen and were loosely based on a computer mouse. *Photo courtesy of Buick*

luxury, or their desire to thumb their nose at any sort of creature comforts. It's where you discover that someone's a techno-geek or an audiophile or a Luddite. It's where you spot the obsessive-compulsives, the symmetry savants, the nostalgists, and the people who insist on doing absolutely everything differently from the way it's ever been done before.

Since this book is all about inspiration, I've rounded up a little of everything. You'll find photos of all kinds of cars from all different eras, with interiors that have been customized in all kinds of ways. Some of these cars are home-built. Some of the interiors were done by local upholstery shops. Some of the cars were completely hand-crafted by big-name builders. And some were built by the automakers with their million-dollar budgets. But you'll find there's a balance here, from low-buck to sky's-the-limit, and from street rods and muscle cars to late-models and 1950s customs.

The best part? What works for a Deuce coupe often looks really cool in a late-model pickup, or a muscle car, or a Honda. The opportunities for cross-pollination—for sharing ideas and inspiration—are really amazing.

In this book, Chapter 1 serves as a sort of overview. It's a survey of some of the wildest, most beautiful, and most attainable cars out there today. Subsequent chapters go into more depth about various parts of the interior: seats and upholstery, trunks, audio systems, floor coverings and headliners, and all kinds of hardware, from knobs and pedals to shifters and door handles.

Once you've found some ideas you love, we'll look at how to turn those ideas into reality. And, finally, there's a resources section at the end so you can reach the companies that have been mentioned throughout the book.

For now, I'd suggest you get out your highlighter or your bookmarks and start turning some pages. If nothing else, I guarantee you'll be both amazed and amused by what you see.

Chapter 1
Custom Looks

There are as many ways to customize a car interior as there are people who want a custom car—or perhaps more, considering how many cars some people build over the course of a lifetime.

Certainly, when it comes to the inside of a vehicle you can change absolutely everything, from the dash to the seats to the carpet to the headliner. And just as certainly,

you can make more subtle—and less expensive—changes, which often have a profound effect on a vehicle's style.

In this chapter, you'll find a sort of survey of what people are doing these days—different styles, different kinds of vehicles, different eras, and, most definitely, different financial investments.

1 This Chip Foose–designed 1936 Ford roadster won both the coveted Ridler Award and America's Most Beautiful Roadster. *Impression*'s completely integrated interior design features a dash that wraps onto the door panels and bright trim pieces that begin on one door and extend around to the other. The unique console houses a stereo head unit. The gauges (from a 1935 Chevy) evoke a vintage airplane design. And aircraft-type canvas, along with pebble leather, adorns the reworked Cobra bucket seats, thanks to Griffin Interiors. *Photo courtesy of Griffin Interiors*

2 Ford's Shelby Cobra concept is not just fluff; it's a ready-to-race roadster. Like that of a vintage Cobra, the instrument panel stretches all the way across the dash. Black and electric blue complement the ample use of aluminum inside. *Photo courtesy of Ford*

3 Lots of people talk about creating private jet–style interiors, but Becker really does so in its JetVan. The company customizes Mercedes-Benz Sprinter vans with aircraft-quality ambient lighting, reclining first-class seats, hide-away work surfaces, gorgeous wood finishes, audiovisual installations, and a choice of floor plans. *Photo courtesy of Becker Automotive Design*

4 Mazda's Hakaze concept was designed to appeal to active, adventurous 30- and 40-somethings. The center console provides mounting brackets for such things as snowboards and wakeboards, and the seats conjure images of oceans and surfing. *Photo courtesy of Mazda*

5 Summit Racing and ProRides set out to build the world's baddest Ford Starliner. The result: this 1961, a.k.a. *SR61*. The instrument panel was narrowed 4 inches, and the console runs the full length of the interior. Bone leather was applied to the custom seats by Appleman Interiors. *Photo courtesy of Summit Racing*

6 This 1929 Ford Model A was built recently to look as if it were put together in 1963. The nostalgia hot rod boasts sweet Tommy the Greek–style pinstriping.

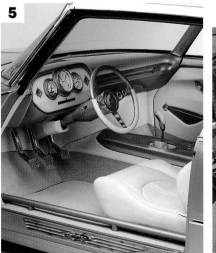

7

8

9

10

11

7 This pristine 1962 Chevrolet Bel Air bubble top named *ShowLow* took home the 2007 Mothers Shine Award. Dig the seriously hefty center console and the hand-fabricated dash. *Photo courtesy of Dennis McClendon*

8 There's no such thing as too much wood. The proof is in this 1934 Ford sedan delivery.

9 Believe it or not, the interior design of this 1955 Chevy Bel Air was inspired by a Mini Cooper. Gabe's Auto Interior covered the seats, dash, door panels, and center console in top-quality leather with incredible, almost-sculptural detailing.

10 The Recovery Room covered a pair of Lexus six-way power bucket seats in Carmel distressed suede with basket-weave inserts, then crafted matching door panels for the 1937 Ford called *Chocolate Thunder*. Rad Rides by Troy built the car, including the handmade waterfall dashboard. The steering wheel is from Billet Specialties. *Photo courtesy of Rad Rides by Troy*

11 Alpine's *Imprint* audio demo car is luxurious. Its cream and brown color scheme is sedate, and the recurring circle theme is soothing. But would you guess it started life as a four-door Mercedes-Benz R500? And the steering wheel? It's on the console, behind the shifter. In fact, you can drive this car from either seat, thanks to twin sets of gas and brake pedals. *Photo courtesy of Alpine Electronics, photography by Carl Edwards*

12 Rick Dore Kustoms built this 1957 Cadillac Eldorado, called *Purple Passion*, with its Wise Guys seats, exquisite custom console, and radically restyled trim pieces. Losing the dash pad was a huge improvement, too.

13 Simple. Lightweight. Lacking in ornamentation. This 1969 Chevy Camaro clearly is all business and race-ready.

14 Symmetry rules the interior of this 1937 Ford cabriolet, from the climate control vents on down to the twin leather-and-velour-covered bucket seats.

15 Climate and sound system controls are located on the driver's "seat wing" in Johnson Controls' re3 concept, where they're easily accessible for both the driver and the front seat passenger. Also check out the cool door-mounted armrest and the 7-inch monitor in the instrument panel. *Photo courtesy of Johnson Controls*

12

13

14

15

16

17

18

19

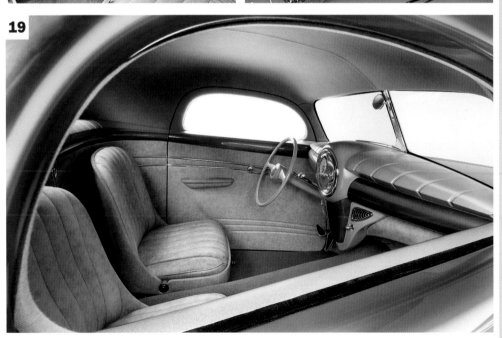

16 The Jeep Compass concept feels both nautical and aeronautical. The outside edges of its stunning seats are covered in leather, while the center section is Goretex with soft-touch grommets. *Photo courtesy of Jeep*

17 This 1934 Chevy coupe is proof that you don't need to spend a lot of money on fancy materials to craft a really clean, attractive interior.

18 How's this for subtle? HiTek Hot Rods outfitted this 1960 Chevy Corvette with a custom molded console and Classic Instruments gauges (the speedo now goes up to 180). Italian Focus Red leather covers the seats and the Budnik steering wheel.

19 Think cars have to be flashy to win big-time awards? Not so. The 2007 Ridler Award went to a car of unusually understated elegance, a 1936 Ford called *First Love* that was built by Rad Rides by Troy and Griffin Interiors. Check out the striking multi-level dash design. *Photo courtesy of Rad Rides by Troy*

20 Absolute Audio's Mercedes-Benz S-Class not only boasts a honkin' big in-dash monitor, it also has a monitor mounted in the middle of the steering wheel.

21 I'd have to call this living room–style seating. Everything about this '42 Lincoln Continental cabriolet oozes comfort and class.

22 Choosing a head-turning accent color can quickly distinguish your ride from the rest. Yellow for the dash trim, suede, and ostrich-look leather really pops in a black Chevy Tahoe interior.

23 What Honda calls purple and blue "glass artwork" really sets off the black and white interior in the company's CR-Z concept car. It should go into production soon, but it's unlikely that the gorgeous gauge and other glass art will make the real-world transition. *Photo courtesy of Honda*

24 This is the all-white-interior version of German tuning house Carlsson Autotechnik's Mercedes-based Carlsson Aigner CK65 RS Blanchimont, built in partnership with German fashion house Etienne Aigner. Carlsson actually offers a choice of 30 interior color combos, plus matching wood trim and a variety of high-tech accessories. *Photo courtesy of Carlsson Autotechnik*

25 The custom console with hydraulic suspension controls blends beautifully with the two-tone but otherwise stock dash in this low rider 1965 Chevy Impala. The striking piping on the upholstery makes the interior particularly appealing.

26 The Chrysler 200C EV concept features an exquisitely sculpted interior. To keep the look clean, there are no dials or switches. The vehicle's controls are accessed through a touch screen on the instrument panel, through a glove box–mounted computer, or through that cool "techno-leaf" in the console, which lets the front passenger adjust personal climate controls and an infotainment system. *Photo courtesy of Chrysler*

27 Hi-Speed Rods & Customs built this 1950 Mercury named *Wasabi*, and Eddie Salcido crafted the stunning green and bright white interior. The VDO Cockpit Royale gauges are a perfect choice, and a monitor is tucked into the console for the Pioneer navigation system and backup camera.

28 Now this is a car—and likely an owner—with personality to spare. The 1960 Volkswagen Beetle actually has a rubber chicken coming through the windshield, a plethora of aftermarket manufacturer stickers that work as a sort of wallpaper, and an obviously checkered past (and present and future).

29 You don't necessarily have to make radical changes to achieve a more luxurious look. In this Mercedes-Benz SL-Class, simply changing the wood trim and adding suede to the seats and dash made a huge difference. Of course, it helps when you start with a high-end Mercedes.

30 Mods to this stunning 1953 Mercury Monterey convertible are surprisingly subtle, such as smoothing the top of the dash pod. More obvious is the change in hardware to fun laminated dash and shift knobs and a simple, smaller steering wheel.

31 This stunning 1932 Ford three-window coupe built by All Ways Hot Rods took home Goodguys' 2008 award for America's Most Beautiful Street Rod. The subtle mesh screens on the dash and console hide part of the surround-sound system.

32 Miles of suede and leather fill the interior of the *Hawaiian Orchid* 1934 Plymouth sedan—especially suede. It covers the console, steering wheel, door panels, and floor. Even the steering column got wrapped in the soft stuff.

33 Simple details and inexpensive materials make for an attractive—and very comfortable—interior in this 1932 Ford three-window coupe.

34 Nothing looks more upscale than white, white, white. Something about the difficulty of keeping it clean implies that you have people for that, as you surely would if you drove—I mean, if you were driven in—the Maybach Landaulet show car. *Photo courtesy of Maybach*

35 Wow. Yummy. There's a lot of texture and high-tech, futuristic luxuriousness going on inside the Mercedes-Benz SLR concept. *Photo courtesy of Mercedes-Benz*

36 A classic black and white and red all over color scheme is all the more striking with pinstriped paint and stitching in this 1991 Chevy Silverado Kustom.

37 You've got to appreciate the simplicity of this 1923 Ford T-bucket. The doorless car still boasts door panel–style treatments with storage pouches, along with a clean dash and the keyhole for the ignition between the seats.

38 Hot Rides by Dean built this 1966 Chevy Chevelle, with its gorgeous custom dash, custom console, and custom seats. The dash has been painted to match the exterior.

39 Sound Choice Audio outfitted this 2007 Saturn Sky with one-off door panels, unique gauge pods on the A-pillar and the top of the windshield, a custom-wrapped dash and interior, and of course plenty of audio gear, including both Pioneer and Fahrenheit CD players.

40 These days, trunks are often just as beautiful, and just as detailed, as passenger compartments. Case in point: the trunk and trunk lid of this Mitch Henderson–designed 1937 Ford roadster, built with help from Stoked Out Specialties.

41 Subtle updates abound inside the *Corpala*, a 1963 Chevy Impala built by Eckert's Rod & Custom that rides on the company's new Torque T3G Chassis with C5 Corvette underpinnings and an LS7 engine. Griffin Interiors applied Rolls-Royce red leather and canvas (to match the canvas exterior top) to the heavily modified factory bucket seats and custom rear seats and also to the smoothed dash.

42 The Toyota FT-HS concept has a skeletal look, with a delta-wing driver's pod and a red driver's seat that tells you who's important here. *Photo courtesy of Toyota*

43

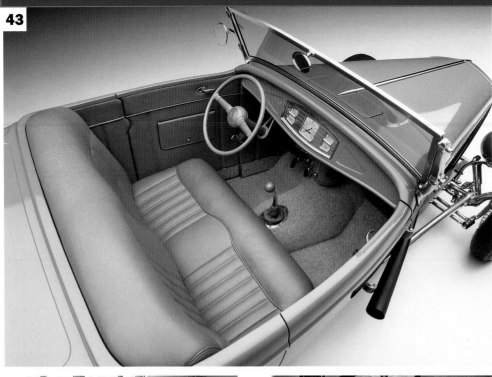

43 Where nostalgic meets progressive: Rad Rides by Troy built this sophisticated 1932 Ford roadster. An instrument cluster from a 1933 Plymouth and a painted Giovanni billet steering wheel look stunning. Griffin Interiors applied buffalo hide over a modified Glide seat and to custom interior panels in a green shade that beautifully complements the paint. *Photo courtesy of Rad Rides by Troy*

44 It's always fun to see a usable back seat in a car with a roll cage. The red-striped upholstery plays up the tubular painted cage and really serves to integrate it with the seating.

45 The mid-engine, Volvo-powered, Caresto V-8 Speedster is a combination sports car/hot rod, a.k.a. *sportrod*. The chestnut brown leather looks gorgeous with the light blue metallic paint, while the steering wheel, gauges, and shifter are Volvo equipment.

46 You don't have to rip everything out of a stock interior to put your imprint on it. This HHR Panel SS concept retains the factory interior pieces; they've just been re-trimmed in striking red and black with white stitching.

44

45

46

47 Custom? Oh, yeah. This 1929 Ford Model A truck is a quintessential rat rod. There's plenty to look at, wouldn't you say?

48 The top of the racing seat beautifully follows the contours of the built-in roll bar on the Pontiac Solstice SD-290 Racer concept. The seat's black leather with red trim and a black perforated section with show-through red make for a striking two-tone execution. Carpet edging and a steering wheel wrap carry through the theme.

49 The curvy interior details—dash, console, door panels, armrest—match beautifully with the curvy exterior of this purple and lavender Willys pickup.

50 Every piece of this 1967 Ford Mustang is brand new, including the body. Classic Design Concepts built the *Flashback* concept, which offers dramatically more head and legroom than a vintage 'Stang. It also sports full instrumentation, supportive seats, and a high-end sound system. Stitched leather sure beats stock vinyl on the dash, and eliminating the factory brightwork really cleaned up the look.

47

48

49

50

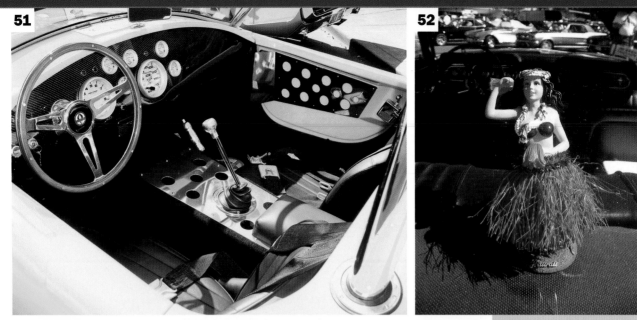

51 Circles are a major styling theme in this 1965 Cobra, which boasts numerous owner-cut sheetmetal trim pieces and a plethora of Auto Meter gauges set into the carbon-fiber dash.

52 How can you not smile at a hula girl dancing on a package shelf or a dash? *Photo by Jody Wetherill*

53 More than 700 hand-shaped pieces went into the *Stallion*, the Chip Foose-designed 1934 Ford three-window coupe that won the Ridler Award. Note the incredible steering wheel, the suede headliner, and the unique upholstery and stitching on the seats, thanks to Griffin Interiors. *Photo courtesy of Griffin Interiors*

1 The power-operated front seat in *Dragzilla* folds flat and mates up with the back seat, turning the entire interior into a bed—the better to watch movies on a large dash-top monitor. Autocore built this stunning Cadillac DeVille, and Interior Shop handled the stitchwork.

Chapter 2
Seats and Upholstery

Perhaps more than any other choices in an interior, the seats and upholstery set the tone and style for a ride. And there certainly are choices far beyond the basic question of bench or buckets. In this chapter, you'll find upholstery without seats and seats without upholstery. Even within the more traditional seating options, there's an inspiring variety of shapes, sizes, styles, colors,

patterns, and textures.

These selections make all the difference in creating a car or truck that offers the ultimate in comfortable long-distance touring, the epitome of luxury, or the barest of minimalism. Plus, seat treatments can go a long way toward establishing a theme, whether the look is retro or space age, rebel or racer, or something truly one-of-a-kind.

2

3

4

5

2 The front buckets and rear love seat in the Ford Reflex concept have exposed, painted, lightweight frames wrapped in mesh. They provide a cool combination of weight savings and increased comfort in hot, humid weather. *Photo courtesy of Ford*

3 When you build a vehicle called the Tiki Truck, clearly it needs tiki mask-style seating. Galpin Auto Sports' multi-colored leather upholstery shows no fear of color or of time. This upholstery was all hand-sewn. *Photo courtesy of Galpin Auto Sports*

4 Leather everywhere—seats, console, armrests, side panels, headliner—creates a truly luxurious look in this 1937 Ford Oze-bodied sedan.

5 Who says the driver's seat and the front passenger seat have to be the same? Scion chose radically different colors for the Hako coupe concept. *Photo courtesy of Scion*

6 Think minivans are for soccer moms? Check out the total nightclub/lounge effect Toyota created in the back of its F3R concept. Plus, the driver's seat rotates to join the party. *Photo courtesy of Toyota*

Who Needs Comfort?

Plushness? Luxury? Highly overrated, at least according to these car owners. Clockwise from left: Tractor seats provide texture and pattern—but no padding—in this Model A, while barely upholstered buckets give the 1934 Chevrolet coupe an old-school racing look. And who would expect a bare-metal bench seat? Good thing the owner of this 1930 Ford carries a can of Anti Monkey Butt, just in case.

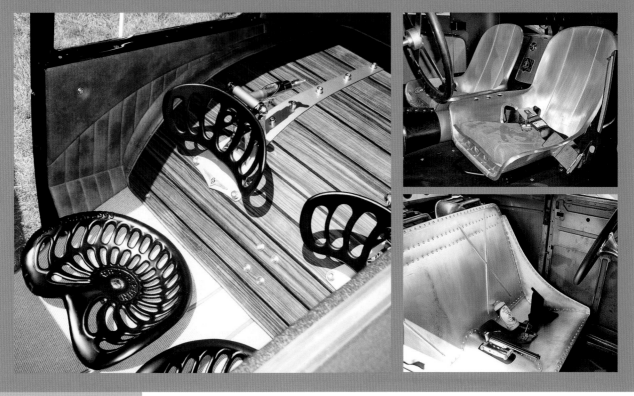

7

8

9

10

11

7 The mix of smooth tan and alligator-style textured leather on the bench seat in this 1941 Plymouth business coupe is plenty sexy, and the matching fold-up armrest makes it possible to seat three—or to let two people get cozy. Upholstering the rest of the interior to match makes the car that much more impressive.

8 This 1937 Chevy coupe may be called *SNSLESS*, but I think scavenging a pair of late-model bucket seats—complete with headrests—is a sensible way to create a ride that's ready for road trips.

9 The Hummer HX concept's interior was inspired by the functional and lightweight elements found in aircraft. Check out the cool seat mounts. *Photo courtesy of Hummer*

10 Simplified stitching really updates the back-seat styling in this 1966 Ford Thunderbird built by Edog Designs. *Photo courtesy of Edog Designs*

11 The Chrysler SR 392 Roadster's seats were inspired by mid-century modern chairs designed by Charles and Ray Eames. *Photo courtesy of Chrysler*

Racing Seats, Then and Now

Racing seats have come a long way since Richard Petty piloted this 1971 Plymouth Road Runner (below). Today, they're not just more stylish, they're considerably more comfortable, even luxurious. Consider the leather-wrapped Recaros in the 1970 Plymouth Barracuda called *Sick Fish* built by Rad Rides by Troy (top right, with an interior by Griffin) and the suede-covered Cobra seats in this 2004 Ford Mustang GT built by Street Concepts.

Photo courtesy of Rad Rides by Troy

Photo courtesy of Street Concepts

12 Stitching, pattern, color, and texture make the seats in Ford's Verve dramatic, but not expensive. The concept car is a pretty close representation of a new small car (smaller than a Focus) that will debut in the United States in 2010.
Photo courtesy of Ford

13 Armand's Auto Upholstery applied miles of butter-yellow leather to the insides of this 1955 Chevy Nomad, on the seats, package shelf, door panels, console, and more. Retaining the factory brightwork was a brilliant move.

14 The roadster's body seems to embrace the driver and passenger seats in this 1941 Willys.

Piping

Contrasting piping can really set off all kinds of different interiors from all different eras, as in (clockwise from top left) a Gasser-style 1941 Willys, a 1961 Ford pickup, a low rider 1965 Chevy Impala, and the Chrysler Imperial concept car.

Photo courtesy of Chrysler

15 Rah, rah, ree! The tiger stripes in this cheerleader-special 1957 Ford are way too cool for school.

16 Just because the seats are right on the floor of this Wild Rod–bodied 1937 Ford doesn't mean they can't be plush and comfortable. Upholstery Unlimited wrapped them in luscious leather. *Photo courtesy of Upholstery Unlimited*

17 Perforations in the black leather reveal orange underneath, which is emphasized by the matching stitching in Galpin Auto Sports' 2007 Ford Fusion called *Turbo Fusion*. Katzkin created the custom leather seat coverings, which match the car's black exterior with orange racing stripes. *Photo courtesy of Galpin Auto Sports*

18 Four different tones—and different textures of leather and suede—really make this low rider 1987 Chevrolet Monte Carlo a standout. Mario's Auto Body did all the work on the car, which appeared on the TV show *Livin' the Low Life. Photo by Jennifer Shields, courtesy of BCII/*Livin' the Low Life

19 Has tweed ever looked more comfortable or more appealing?

20 Airstream's iconic RV designs and the 1960s cult film *2001: A Space Odyssey* were inspirations for the Ford Airstream concept. Arne Jacobsen's iconic *Egg* chair even appeared in the movie, and it clearly inspired these swiveling front captain's chairs. The rear seating provides more of a lounge vibe. *Photo courtesy of Ford*

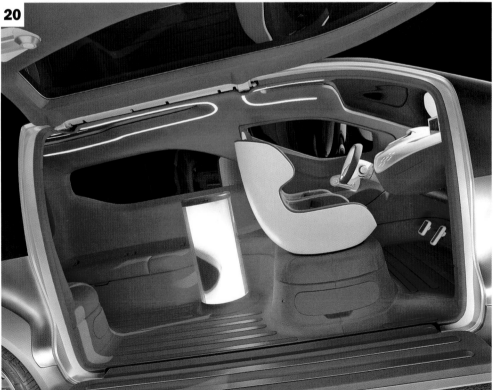

Couch-Style Back Seats

Automakers—particularly those with a share of the sport compact market—have been designing couch-style back seats for their concept cars. The comfy design certainly has its appeal, as in the Scion Fuse (left) and the Mazda Ryuga (right).

Photo courtesy of Scion

Photo courtesy of Mazda

21 Comfort clearly was not the goal when Alpine Electronics built a ribbed Plexiglas solo seat for this outrageous Mini Cooper S.

22 These sheetmetal interior panels and bomber-style bucket seats were designed to look like a slightly refined B-29 airplane. They're home-built, too. This Deuce is called *Red Ram Special*, and see how the back of the body looks like bare metal? It's actually painted fiberglass.

23 Plaid is downright shocking—and outrageously fun—in this 1947 Chevrolet Fleetliner built by POSIES. *Photo courtesy of POSIES*

24 Are these the wildest headrests you've ever seen? You know they are. That's a 1960 VW Beetle, in case you're wondering.

Bench Seat Options

Remember when bench seats were for your dad's car and all the cool kids had buckets? Well, there are plenty of ways to make bench seats cool these days. Clockwise from top left: You can do a bench bottom with bucket seat–style backrests, like this Fesler Built 1967 Chevy pickup. You can do a bench-style backrest with a split bottom, as in the Blastolene B-702. You can do a split back with nicely integrated his-and-hers armrests, like this Wise Guys seat in a 1951 Chevy pickup. You can turn the entire interior into a molded-in plush bench, like this decadent 1932 Ford highboy. Or you can add lumbar and thigh supports, along with great stitching and contrasting trim, as in this swoopy 1936 Plymouth.

Photo courtesy of Fesler Built

25 Dan's Auto Upholstery wrapped the late-model buckets in smooth black and pleated cream leather for the 1957 Chevy Bel Air called *Black Mamba*. Note the thigh bolsters—a great choice for a daily driver or a long-haul tourer. And side bolsters were a particularly wise move for this car, with its supercharged Dodge Viper V-10.

26 A pair of beautifully dressed bucket seats snuggle up close in this 1934 Ford three-window coupe.

27 That's actual Rawlings baseball glove leather—the same stuff Major League Baseball (MLB) players use—on the seats of this 2008 Chevy Tahoe. The truck was built for AutoTrader.com, and it was the grand prize in the Turn2 game on the MLB.com website. *Photo courtesy of AutoTrader.com*

28 Automakers have been installing thinner and thinner seats in concept cars of late. The single-touch stackable seats in the Ford Explorer America concept appear to float, since they're not actually anchored to the floor. Instead, they're connected to the base of the center console. *Photo courtesy of Ford*

Stitching Details

With the advent of computer-controlled sewing machines, it's much easier to add virtually any design—from a name to a highly detailed logo—to your upholstery. The stitching can even add dimension, as in this 1964 Chevy Chevelle with Super Sport logos. That pretty two-headed design graces the seats in Galpin Auto Sports' *Warriors in Pink* Mustang.

Photo courtesy of Galpin Auto Sports

29 This 1969 Chevy Camaro took home Goodguys' 2008 Street Machine of the Year award. *Razor* was built by Ringbrothers, which has its own line of stainless-steel fasteners. Upholstery Unlimited used those fasteners as a styling detail throughout the Hunter leather interior, including on the seats. *Photo courtesy of Upholstery Unlimited*

30

31

32

33

30 Retro is way cool with glitter white vinyl, silver welting, and silver buttons set into the red diamond pleating inside this rat rod. The seat even looks pretty comfy.

31 This sort of upholstery treatment would look great in a car with a two-tone paint job. While Ford's Forty-Nine concept is all black outside, the seats wear a striking combination of black and sienna leather. *Photo courtesy of Ford*

32 Chrysler's Town & Country Black Jack concept is literally set up to be a casino on wheels. The dealer gets that center, rear-facing seat. And the players can rest comfortably on the curvy banquette. LEDs light up the floor and the clear-topped gaming table, which is rimmed in carbon fiber. *Photo courtesy of Chrysler*

33 Max's Upholstery crafted custom bucket seats that swivel at the touch of a button for this stunning 1939 Chevy Master Deluxe low rider, which is called *Maldito 1939.* They're swathed in green velvet with biscuit tufting, coffin pleats, and yellow velvet welting. *Photo by Jennifer Shields, courtesy of BCII/Livin' the Low Life*

Disappearing Seat Bottoms

Toyota's A-BAT pickup truck concept features inspiring seating. For starters, the rear seat bottoms retract to increase cargo flexibility within the cab. Also, high-end mountain bike frames inspired designers to leave structural elements exposed inside; the front seats' bare frames look particularly great from the rear.

Photos courtesy of Toyota

31

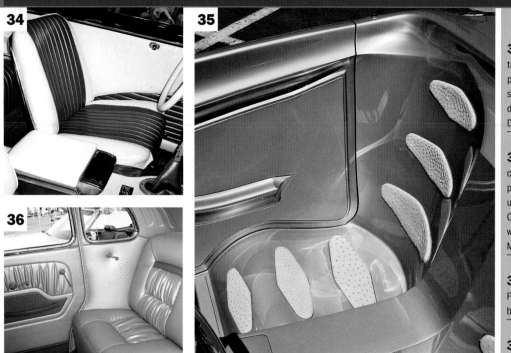

34 Smooth white leather and tuck-and-roll purple with silver piping make for some memorable seats in this 1954 Ford Victoria designed by Kaucher Kustoms. Downtown Willy crafted the interior.

35 Who needs seats when you can custom fabricate metal interior panels and add a dash of ostrich upholstery? Scott's Hotrods 'n' Customs built this 1932 Ford, which nabbed the 2008 America's Most Beautiful Roadster award.

36 The shiny vinyl in this 1935 Ford sedan looks a lot like satin, but it's far more durable.

37 Faurecia, a supplier to the automakers, used a mix of colors and materials to create an upscale look for the seats in the Premium Attitude concept car. The silk fabric–like finish on the back of the seats is actually real wood veneer. *Photo courtesy of Faurecia*

38 Mexican blankets have long been a popular and cheap seat-covering material, but they're taken to a new—and even wipe-clean—level in this wild 1924 Dodge Brothers sedan.

39 Pinstriping looks striking on vinyl upholstery in this 1965 Chevy C-10 pickup.

40 Beautiful grille-design inserts in the seats match the speaker faces beyond, while roll bar–style headrests add a sporty touch in this 1937 Chevy built by Kindig-It Design and JS Custom Interior. The coupe won the 2007 SEMA Design Award for Best GM Hot Rod.

41 The funky race-inspired seats in the Audi R8 V12 TDI concept have an almost Egyptian—or alien—quality. *Photo courtesy of Audi*

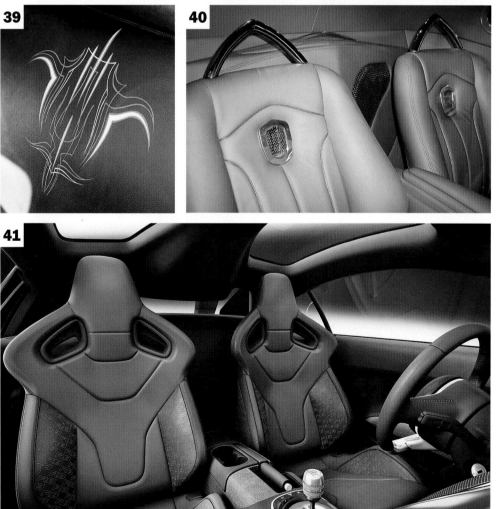

42 Galpin Auto Sports created a sort of *Mad Max* look for the seats in its *Armageddon Truck.* Various colors of leather have been torn, stressed, and then sewn together patchwork-style. *Photo courtesy of Galpin Auto Sports*

43 Heated and cooled thigh supports come out from under the second-row seats, and footrests deploy rearward from the front seats so passengers can fully recline in the Lincoln MKT concept. *Photo courtesy of Lincoln*

44 How about molding a car's interior around bucket seats in the back? This plush, three-tone look—complete with side bolsters—is particularly wild for a muscle car. Wrocket Products is responsible for this 1967 Chevy Nova's interior.

45 Even stock Mercury Mariner seats can look radical when you opt for two different textures and fabrics: in this case, basic black leather paired with eye-popping leopard-print furry cowhide. *Photo courtesy of Mercury*

46 Seatbacks painted to match the exterior look hot in this 1955 Chevy Bel Air.

Rumble Seats

It really is possible to create a variety of looks, even within the relatively small confines of a rumble seat. Adding speakers for the way-back passengers is a thoughtful touch, too.

47 John D'Agostino Kustom Kars jazzed up this 2008 Chrysler Sebring with help from Bob Divine Interiors. Even though the back seat is a bench, it got the same upholstery treatment as the buckets for a cohesive look.

48 The single and double pleating in this Range Rover Sport forms a cool sort of plaid.

49 Exposed support structure and circular stitching make the seats in this 1932 Ford roadster appear deceptively simple. Hollywood Hot Rods built the car.

Ready-to-Install Seat Coverings

Photo courtesy of Katzkin

Several companies offer stitched-to-fit, ready-to-install leather coverings for a plethora of seats. Katzkin has one of the largest selections when it comes to materials, including 59 standard leathers, plus Suedezkin simulated suede and leather that's been textured to look like alligator, lizard, ostrich, and carbon fiber.

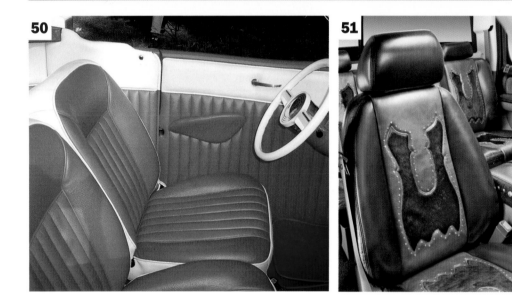

50 A contrasting color on the sides—and stitching that lines up in both the white and red areas—makes all the difference on an otherwise simple seat in this 1935 Ford roadster.

51 It's more than a little bit country. The Country Music Chevrolet Silverado HD pickup gets its Nashville styling from a blend of leathers—specifically Spinneybeck Lucente black gloss, Edelman Cowboy black tooled, Edelman Proper English Ale, Edelman Cavallini cow hair, and Artisian Redwood. *Photo courtesy of Chevrolet*

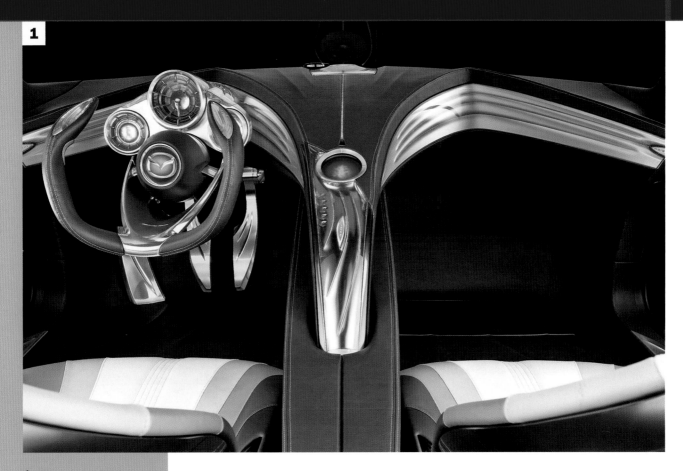

1 Mazda pared dashboard design down to the barest essentials, then made it sensual, stimulating, and incredibly sporty through the use of leather and polished aluminum in the Ryuga concept. The open-top steering wheel provides an unobstructed view of the gauges. *Photo courtesy of Mazda*

Chapter 3
Dashboards and Gauges

The dashboard typically is the place where a driver gets necessary information—things like speed, engine rpm, fuel level, water temperature, time of day. But a dashboard is so much more. It's quite literally the focal point of any interior.

And as you'll see here, dash designs range from straight and simple to molded and swoopy. A dash can tie into the center console or wrap around onto the doors, or it can stand alone. And of course it can feature a mix of materials, such as metal, wood, vinyl, leather, and suede.

In terms of function, the dashboard can be home to *all* of a vehicle's controls, including those for the climate control and sound systems. Or it can be nearly bare of decoration and instrumentation.

Gauges, too, offer tremendous opportunity for self-expression, from their mounting locations to their designs. You can choose different background colors, different bezels, or different type styles. You can choose individual gauges or multi-function gauges. You can go analog or digital. You can treat gauges as key design elements on a dash or tuck them discreetly away from passengers' prying eyes.

2 A full complement of Auto Meter gauges looks so right in the dash of this 1963 Chevrolet Corvette.

3 The chrome gauge cluster in this 1939 Ford captures the glamour of the golden age of flying.

4 Do you suppose every gauge monitors something different? Those are all Stewart Warner Maximum Performance gauges ringing the obviously custom dash of this 1967 Mini Cooper truck. *Photo courtesy of CarSponsorships.com*

A Single Center-Mounted Gauge

Each of these spectacular automobiles boasts a single multi-function gauge in the center of its dash, which looks remarkably like a fine watch. Rad Rides by Troy crafted the 1937 Ford convertible on the left, called *Chocolate Thunder*, with its one-piece clock, speedometer, and odometer with Classic Instruments mechanicals. The Blastolene B-702 (center) sports more of a chronograph style out of a Lincoln Zephyr, while the 1937 Chevy coupe built by Kindig-It Design features an all-in-one cluster.

Photo courtesy of Rad Rides by Troy

5 You don't have to make radical changes—or spend radical money—to create a seriously customized look, as proven by the attention-getting green trim inside this DSO Eyewear Honda Element.

6 This 1962 Chevy Bel Air features custom gauges from Classic Instruments in a hand-fabricated dash—two of the many reasons *ShowLow* took home a Boyd Coddington Pro's Pick award.

7 The wild-looking multi-level instrument panel in the Scion t2B concept not only provides digital readouts of things such as speed, rpm, and gear selection, it also includes a large information ticker with access to movies, games, and music downloads. *Photo courtesy of Scion*

8 The unbelievably unique dash in the *Tubester*, which started life as a 1933 Ford pickup, was actually formed using laminated wood.

9 Texturized stainless looks sexy in a Model A Ford.

10 Can you spot the only stock parts on the now-fiberglass dash of this owner-built 1996 Chevy S-10 Blazer? Yep, the headlight controls are the last vestiges of Chevydom. Love the pinstriping.

11 With luscious leather and beautiful brightwork, this dash looks poised to take flight.

12 Changing from faux wood to silver and swapping from factory gauges to Auto Meter units really changes the look of a 1969 Ford Mustang instrument panel.

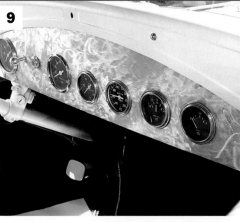

Inserts to Replace Stock Instruments

Many companies—including Sun Spec Billet Factory, Haneline, and Brothers—make billet and engine-turned metal inserts to fit inside the factory instrument panel of a wide variety of cars and trucks, including this 1954 Chevy. The inserts let you back-mount standard-size gauges from such companies as VDO, Auto Meter, and Classic Instruments for a professionally installed look. Some of the panels even come with gauges already installed.

13

14

15

16

13 I love seeing a street rod treatment in a late-model. The top of this Dodge Charger's dash is completely custom, and the new piece was painted to match the exterior. The bottom portion got a full suede treatment, as did the center of the steering wheel. The new instrument cluster housing has a trio of gauges instead of the factory four-pack.

14 Street & Performance's 1957 Chevy sports Dakota Digital gauges in a smoothed factory instrument panel. The two-tone DuPont Hot Hues paint looks particularly slick.

15 An arc of gauges forms a sculptural centerpiece in this 1955 Chevy Bel Air, with its clean, leather-wrapped dash.

16 The instrument cluster actually floats in front of the dash in Ford's Super Chief concept. *Photo courtesy of Ford*

17 The stunning gauges in the 1966 Chevy Biscayne called *Hurricayne* were made by Classic Instruments. Rad Rides by Troy installed brushed aluminum bezels to match the rest of the interior detailing, including the vent surrounds. *Photo courtesy of Rad Rides by Troy*

Console-Mounted Gauges

One way to keep the dash looking clean and uncluttered is to mount some of your gauges on the center console, as in (clockwise from top left) a 1969 Chevrolet Z/28 Camaro called *OutRayJus*, a 1991 Chevy Silverado Kustom pickup, and a sueded-out 1941 Willys.

18 All the vinyl was stripped off the dash of this 1967 Cadillac Coupe DeVille and the upper portion was painted body color—green with major metalflake—then it was beautifully pinstriped. The filled factory instrument panel now sports Auto Meter Arctic White Series gauges.

19 Gauge-face kits are available to change the look of a variety of late-model vehicles, including this GMC pickup.

20 Attention to detail defines this 1939 Chevy town sedan, with a character line that travels across the top of the dash and around the doors, with circles that play out with pleasing symmetry, and with an orange-painted gauge panel that picks up the car's exterior color. The gauges' yellow backlit centers also add some intrigue.

Mascots

You're never alone with (from left) the Bone-ster, Ed "Big Daddy" Roth's Rat Fink, or a scary skull. Clearly, a painted-on passenger can set the tone for a ride.

21 *DUB Magazine* customized this Pepsi Street Motion Dodge Nitro, which sports a radical new dash. Dig the way-cool steering wheel with the suede horn button.

22 Would you believe this is a 1957 Chevy Bel Air? The dash came out of a Gen II Dodge Viper—to go along with the Paxton-supercharged Viper V-10 under the hood! She's called *Black Mamba*, and she's definitely a wild child.

23 The sweeping curve of the dash embraces the substantial center console in this 1950 Mercury called *Mercules*.

24 *Undisputed* boasts a remarkably clean and pretty dash/console combo. Scott's Hotrods 'n' Customs placed the gauges on the 1932 Ford's center stack to create a satisfying symmetry. A touch-open panel on the console hides a starter button, a toggle switch that controls the main power for the vehicle, a switch for the headlights, and a switch to raise and lower the trunk lid.

25 Metalcrafters fabricated the painted dash/center console in this 1966 Chevy Impala, and Upholstery Unlimited made it truly fabulous with 2008 Chrysler textured fabric and Ringbrothers fasteners. *Photo courtesy of Upholstery Unlimited*

26 Incredible airbrushing makes this 1937 Ford coupe's dash and waterfall console unforgettable. Note the oval styling theme on the vents, the Vintage Air control panel, the brake pedal, and the door handles.

27 Autographs by such hot rodding notables as Gene Winfield, Ed "Big Daddy" Roth, and Pat Ganahl graffiti the dash of this 1928 Ford.

Dash-Top Gauges

You could go the traditional route and mount a freestanding tach on top of the dash, as in this 1964 Ford Falcon Sprint convertible (left). Or you could mount a gauge pod from Classic Design Concepts on top of your dash, as Street Concepts did in this 2007 Mustang GT (center). Another option: Swap your stock dash pad for one of these units from Just Dashes that includes an angled triple gauge pod, as in the Chevy pickup (right; this pad fits 1967–1972 Chevrolets and GMCs).

Photo courtesy of Just Dashes

28 The instrument panel in this 1961 Ford Starliner was welded, filled, and narrowed 4 inches, and it's now home to Auto Meter Arctic White Series gauges. ProRides built the *SR61* for Summit Racing. *Photo courtesy of Summit Racing*

29 Classic Instruments' gauges look particularly striking in red, white, and gray in a 1934 Chevy dash.

30 Pillar pods—like those from Auto Meter—make it easy to install gauges on the A-pillar of a lot of vehicles, including this 1965 Ford Mustang.

31 Mounting gauges so they're angled upward makes all kinds of sense for a tall driver, as in this 1941 Ford Deluxe Coupe.

32 An AC Schnitzer carbon-fiber interior kit really dresses up the dash, console, shift knob, and steering wheel in CEC's BMW 335 coupe.

Direct Replacements

If you want or need new gauges—and particularly if you'd like more instrumentation without radically changing the look of your stock instrument panel—you can go with a set of direct replacements. They can be vehicle-specific, such as the Classic Instruments gauge packages for (clockwise from top left) a 1956 and a 1957 Chevy Bel Air. Or, if you're really lucky, you can find standard gauges that fit your bezels, such as the VDO gauges in this 1948 Chevy Fleetline.

33 This curvy handmade aluminum dash looks like a piece of art deco furniture, with its stunning wood trim and beautifully framed Haneline gauges. POSIES created this extraordinary 1929 Ford pickup called *ThunderRoad*. *Photo courtesy of POSIES*

33

Digital Gauges

There are so many ways to go digital these days. You can install a complete replacement gauge cluster or swap individual digital gauges in place of factory analog units, as in (top row, from left): a 1970 Chevrolet Chevelle SS from Fesler Built, a 1956 Ford truck, and a 1961 Chevy Corvette. Or you can opt for universal components and create your own dash composition using gauges from manufacturers such as Dakota Digital and Nordskog.

Photo courtesy of Fesler Built

Photo courtesy of Fesler Built

Photo courtesy of Nordskog

Stick-On Graphics

Here's a fun and easy way to personalize a late-model Mini Cooper: Mini USA has partnered with a company called Original Wraps to offer custom-fit, stick-on, 3M vinyl dash graphics. Designs range from original art to national flags. You can even upload a photo or create your own design. In time, Original Wraps likely will offer these graphics for all kinds of vehicles.

34 Rad Rides by Troy sculpted a stunning dash out of carbon fiber to complement the exterior of this 1940 Ford called *Vision*. Classic Instruments crafted the custom gauges, which reveal their internals like high-end watches. A Kenwood touchscreen head unit sits in the center of the dash, flanked by a pair of speakers. Bob Thrash at Rad Rides deserves design credit, while Griffin Interiors covered the power bucket seats with a combination of canvas and Edelman shrunken buffalo hides. *Photo courtesy of Rad Rides by Troy*

35 Sound Choice Audio built the custom dash for this 1979 Pontiac Trans Am with the gauges offset to the right of the driver.

34

35

36 "Squircles"—Ford design-speak meaning squares with rounded-off corners—are a unifying theme inside the Interceptor concept. The dash trim, gauges, steering wheel, horn button, seat trim, and even the shifter housing are all squircles. *Photo courtesy of Ford*

37 Pyramid Street Rods set out to create a sort of "gentleman's altered" look in this 1932 Ford roadster. It features a modified Ron White dash with Classic Instruments gauges.

38 Chevrolet tapped Rage Imports to build this radical Aveo for the 2007 SEMA Show. The *Green Monster* sports a carbon fiber-wrapped dash and, of course, an iPod interface. The factory sound system and climate control have been deleted—clues that this is not just a pretty face; it's a completely tuned performance vehicle.

Underdash Gauges

One of the easiest spots to add more gauges is under the dash—on either side of the steering wheel. You can mount them independently, like the Mopar units in this 1968 Dodge Dart (left). Or you can install them in a gauge panel, like this 1969 Dodge Coronet R/T that was built as a Sunpro sweepstakes giveaway car.

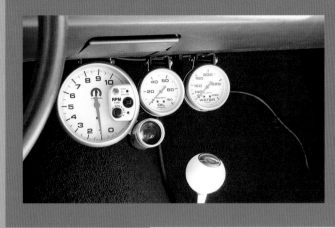

Photo courtesy of Sunpro

39 Cool bezels give these unique gauges a real compass look and play up the theme of the Jeep Compass concept. *Photo courtesy of Jeep*

40 Swapping from factory black-face gauges to custom cream units (adorned with the Vasser Chevrolet dealership logo) really warmed up the interior in this 1962 Chevy Impala. Dominator Street Rods built the car for Jim Vasser and son Jimmy, the Champ Car racer.

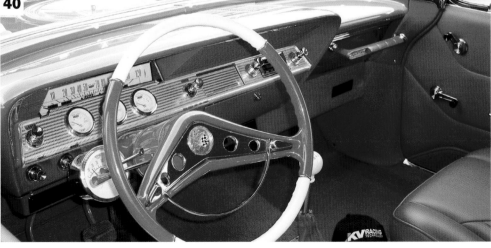

41

41 The clean, painted dash—with its swoopy center stack—matches the two-tone/pinstriped exterior of this 1937 Ford. Dakota Digital gauges in one of the company's universal street rod panels have been Frenched into the dash.

42 Ringbrothers aimed for a sleek European look for the interior of the Roush Reactor 1967 Ford Mustang, which won Goodguys' 2007 Street Machine of the Year award.

43 The low and elegant leather-wrapped dash on the Ford Fairlane concept appears to open up and offer the driver a sneak peak at the gauges, which are located beneath a panel of oak and maple bentwood laminate. Also note how the clean, geometric console breaks into the dash. *Photo courtesy of Ford*

42

43

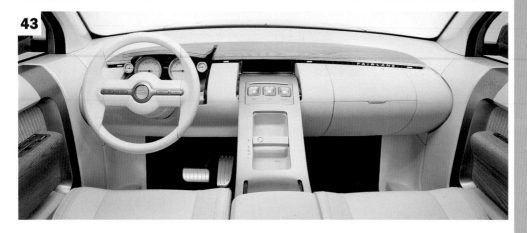

44 Murals have been making a comeback. That's some seriously fine art on the dash of this 1961 Ford pickup.

45 Mark III Customs added the ash wood to the dash of this 2008 Chevy Tahoe. That's the same wood Rawlings uses to make Major League Baseball bats. The truck was built for AutoTrader.com, and after 220 current Major League baseball players autographed the hood, Barrett-Jackson auctioned it off to benefit youth baseball programs. *Photo courtesy of AutoTrader.com*

46 Fesler outfitted this 1949 Merc with way-cool Bonspeed Roulette gauges. *Photo courtesy of Fesler Built*

Doing the Deuce

For the most part, Deuce dashboards inspire symmetry, much like the original styling. Of course, occasionally someone breaks the trend and does something really crazy, such as installing a glove box. Here's a look at a few different ways you can do up a Deuce.

Photo courtesy of POSIES

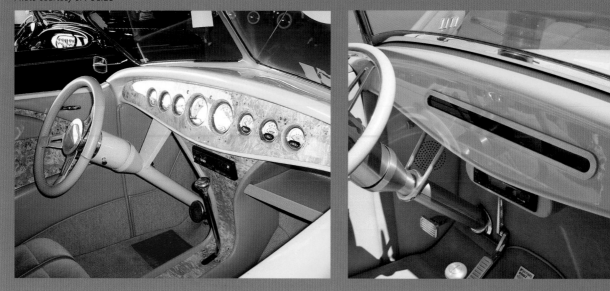

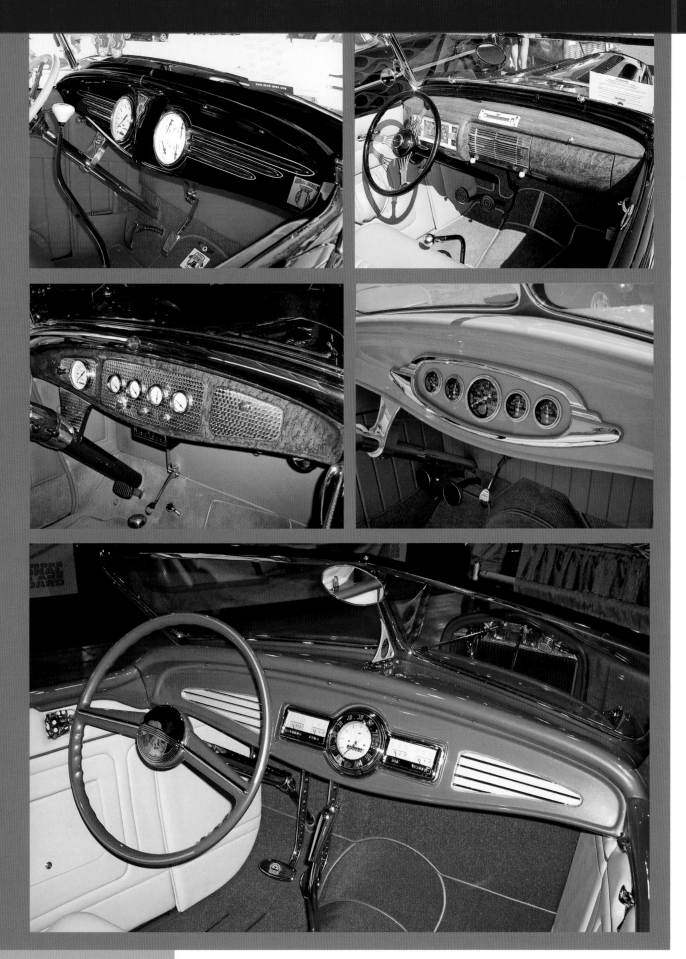

Chapter 4
Door Panels

Door panels are often upholstered to match the seats, as well as the rest of the panels in an interior. But they certainly can go beyond basic upholstery, with sculptural elements, stunning armrests, attention-getting grab handles, and so much more. In fact, many top-notch builders are wrapping the dash design around onto the doors these days, truly integrating them into the entire interior design. Still, there's a lot to be said for elegant simplicity and practicality.

2 Suede, leather, and carpet do a beautiful job of tying together interior styling themes in this 1932 Ford three-window coupe.

3 Is it daring to use suede on an armrest? It certainly could show wear. But oh, is it beautiful. This sweet ride is the *Hawaiian Orchid*, a 1934 Plymouth sedan.

4 Clearly, this 1965 Chevrolet El Camino is no work truck. The ample leather pleating on the door panels—and the seats—looks absolutely opulent.

5 The Caresto Volvo-powered V-8 Speedster features hand-stitched Scottish chestnut leather in its immaculate interior.

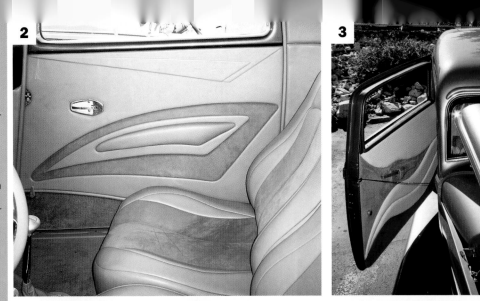

Pleasingly Pleated

Evenly spaced, vertical pleats can provide a traditional hot rod look, as they do in a 1932 Ford roadster (top left) and a 1930 Ford Model A pickup (right), while the stock door panel on this 1955 Chevy Cameo pickup benefits from leather trim that's been pleated to match the bench seat.

6 Think plumbing materials inspired the look for *Project Supernova*, Goodguys' 2009 Grand Prize Giveaway car? Precision Coachworks built the 1970 Chevy Nova, which features a Tiger Cage bolt-in stainless-steel roll cage and a mighty similar-looking tubular armrest.

7 Curvaceous doesn't even begin to describe the molded mania inside this 1933 Ford pickup called the *Tubester*. Believe it or not, those door panels are made from laminated sycamore, maple, walnut, and sugar pine.

8 Alligator-style leather is making waves in this 1941 Plymouth business coupe, with its subtly shaped armrest.

Door Panels and Beyond

In many cases, a door panel's styling is part of a larger interior theme that extends well beyond the door panel itself. Sometimes it extends forward, sometimes rearward, and sometimes both. Consider (clockwise from right) this RodBods stretched 1932 Ford roadster done by Gabe's Street Rods Custom Interiors, a 1932 Ford with an ostrich-and-leather combo, another stunning Deuce, a 1936 Plymouth that won a Meguiar's Magnificent Masterpiece award, and a 1939 Ford roadster.

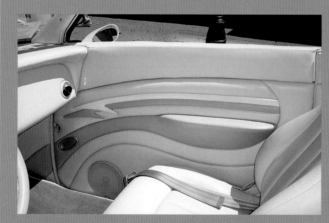

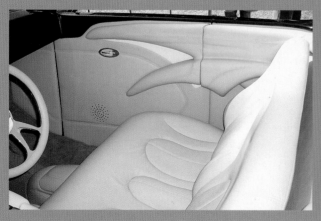

9 The Western styling theme clearly extends to the door panel in this 1933 Ford with a Speedstar body and an interior by Upholstery Unlimited. *Photo courtesy of Upholstery Unlimited*

10 The black trim on the door panel and beyond references the outside styling of this 1957 Buick Special. The armrest also flows straight back from the door panel to the rear seat area.

11 It's always fun to see traditional hot rod styling in a very untraditional place, like a 2007 Hyundai Azera. Street Concepts added the suede with silver stitching and old-school quilting. *Photo courtesy of Street Concepts*

12 This 1937 Oze-bodied Ford is known as *Bad to the Bone*. The textured leather really picks up the range of hues expressed by the paint. Auto Upholstery Unlimited handled the stunning interior work.

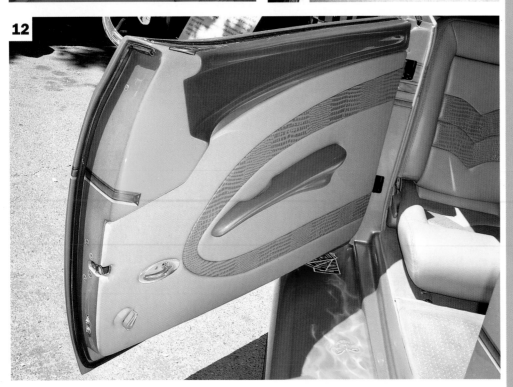

13

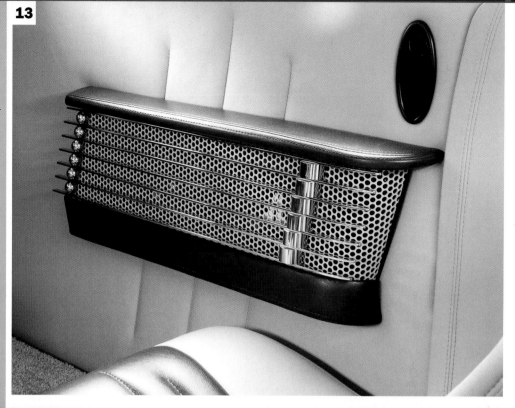

13 POSIES has crafted perhaps the most beautiful armrest ever. This jukebox-style jewel adorns the inside of the 1937 *Extremeliner*. *Photo courtesy of POSIES*

Bare Minimalist Looks

There's something pure and appealing about a bare metal door. It's honest. It's plain-spoken. And, in the case of this 1931 rat rod open-top coupe (top left), it's rusting to a lovely patina, too. The other naked door panels belong to a Shadow Rods lengthened 1927 Ford (right), and Spectre Performance's 1970 Chevy El Camino.

14 The back seat area gets a door panel–style treatment in this very comfortable-looking 1932 Ford Tudor sedan.

15 Brightwork really spices up the styling in this 1955 Chevy Bel Air, and so does a mix of smooth and perforated leather.

16 Eddie Salcido crafted the immaculate interior for this stunning 1950s-style custom called *Wasabi*. The 1950 Merc even has name badges on its door panels.

17 What a difference you can make with a little hot-pink suede and glittery replacements for the factory woodgrain trim pieces. West Coast Customs pimped out this Porsche Cayenne for Kat of the TV show *My Super Sweet 16*.

18 Graffiti door panels are a perfect fit in this endearingly crazy 1960 Volkswagen Beetle. Gotta say: Whiteboard *is* an easy and economical way to go.

Storage Spaces

When you really drive a car, you can never have too much storage space. Here are a few cool storage solutions in a pair of 1932 Ford roadsters and a 1933 (center). Upholstery Unlimited handled the door panels on the latter.

Photo courtesy of Upholstery Unlimited

19 The elegantly sculpted and chromed armrest really sets off the multi-color, multi-texture door panel in this incredible slammed 1951 Mercury. Her name is *Ruby Begonia*, and she's the unofficial mascot of Galvin Precision Machining.

20 Panoz completely redesigned the door panels—and far more—in this 1965 Ford Mustang for actor Patrick Dempsey (star of the TV show *Grey's Anatomy*), going for a thoroughly modern look with suede, leather, and stainless.

21 Fesler hand-formed this sleek armrest out of steel, then topped it off with leather for this 1969 Chevy Blazer. The curve nicely echoes the door handle. *Photo courtesy of Fesler Built*

19

20

21

Dash Integration

Wrapping the dashboard around so that it seems to continue right onto the door panels unifies a vehicle's interior in a dramatic, built-like-the-big-guys-do-it kind of way. Perfect examples are (from top) a 1937 Ford called *Chocolate Thunder* built by Rad Rides by Troy, Mitch Henderson's 1937 Ford roadster that was a runner-up for Goodguys' 2008 America's Most Beautiful Street Rod award, and an incredible 1955 Chevy Bel Air.

Photo courtesy of Rad Rides by Troy

22 The wood and stainless door handle and trim beautifully match the seat detailing and the dash in this 1949 Packard, better known as *Packrat*.

Similar But Not Matching

Nobody says all the door panels in a vehicle have to be exactly the same. In the Hummer HX concept (top), the driver-side door features a built-in flashlight and first aid kit, while the passenger-side door features a similarly styled shovel. And in Faurecia's Premium Attitude concept, styling for the front and rear door panels is likewise similar but by no means the same. (Dig the cool armrest storage compartment, too.)

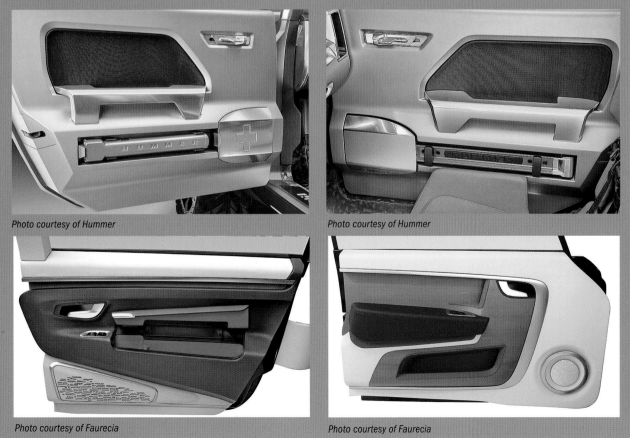

Photo courtesy of Hummer

Photo courtesy of Hummer

Photo courtesy of Faurecia

Photo courtesy of Faurecia

Flame It

Flames are an ever-popular hot rod styling theme, and they can look particularly hot on a door panel, whether you opt for a two-tone or a monochrome look. Carrying a torch are (clockwise from top left) a 1931 Ford sedan, a 1972 Chevy Chevelle, a 1932 Ford three-window coupe, and a 1955 Chevy 150 two-door sedan.

23 The Country Music Chevy Silverado concept truck features a bevy of cowboy-style leather in different colors and textures. Check out the nail-head stud detailing on the armrest.

24 Professionally built cars don't have to use expensive materials. Upholstery Unlimited applied smooth and textured fabric—no leather—to the door panels and interior of this 1966 Chevrolet Impala. Love the grab handle. *Photo courtesy of Upholstery Unlimited*

25 The interior in this Plymouth is all about texture, plus a pleasing repetition of oval shapes for the climate control vents and the door handles. Jon Lind Interiors handled the work for the *Waza '49*.

26 Several companies, including EZ Boy Interiors, offer panel board interior kits. The panels come pre-cut to fit a particular vehicle, like this Deuce kit, and they're ready to be upholstered.

27 When a car's interior is all about smooth, painted metal, it makes sense to have a matching swoopy armrest, don't you think? In this case, the car is the Scott's Hotrods 'n' Customs-built 1932 Ford that won the 2008 America's Most Beautiful Roadster award.

28 A combination of pinstriping, billet, and flames defines the customized interior of this low rider GMC Sierra.

Cargo Area Doors

The cargo area door for a sedan delivery offers a nice big canvas for expression and a chance to match or contrast with the vehicle's other door panels. Some particularly nice looks include those (from left) on a 1948 Chevy, a 1932 Ford (winner of Goodguys' 2008 Street Rod of the Year award), and a 1939 Chevy.

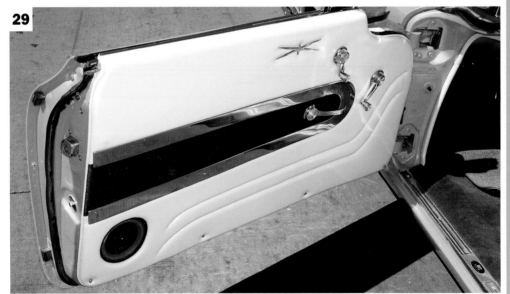

29 Fun 1950s-style trim really sets off the totally custom door panel in this 1959 Pontiac Bonneville.

30 Heavily textured leather, smooth leather, and snakeskin make for a stunning door panel that matches the bench seat in this 1951 GMC pickup.

31 Chrysler's Mopar Underground SEMA design team and Quality Metalcraft (QMC) built the SR 392 Roadster with the world's first-ever steel reproduction of a 1927 street rod body (the Shadow Rods XL-27, stamped by QMC). They let the mechanicals show and chose durable materials as a way to pay homage to Motor City, the industrial backbone of Detroit.

32 Standout looks come from the mix of ostrich, leather, and that hot red paint. The armrest also ties into the dash design. Rivero Upholstery did all the stitching inside this 1939 Chevy coupe called *O-Henry*.

33 Yards and yards of Baked Bean leather grace the inside of this 1966 Chevy Biscayne dubbed *Hurricayne*. The stainless trim may have all been removed from the outside, but it looks striking indoors alongside that matching door handle. Rad Rides by Troy built the car, and Griffin Interiors handled the inside. *Photo courtesy of Griffin Interiors*

34 Meticulous craftsmanship helped this 1939 Chevy coupe win Best of Show at the Eldorado/ Silverado hotels during Hot August Nights 2008.

Armrest/Storage Two-Fer

Ford stashed extra storage space inside the fold-down armrests for the second row of seats in the Fairlane SUV concept. You can access the storage compartments when the armrests are in their up position.

Photos courtesy of Ford

1 You've gotta love the way the driver side of this gorgeous dashboard sweeps into the console. Truly spectacular! And would you guess it's a 1967 Chevy Nova? Wrocket Products is responsible for the *Killer 67 Nova-Star*'s interior, which wears DuPont Hot Hues paint in Champagne Fizz and Candy Molten Orange to match the exterior. The oval digital gauges are a beautiful complement to the Vintage Air controls, too.

Chapter 5
Consoles

These days, we practically take consoles for granted. Can you even think of a new vehicle that doesn't have some sort of center console? So if you plan to drive a vintage ride on a regular basis, it's certainly nice to outfit it with something comparable, perhaps even a design that has ample storage space inside and cupholders, too.

Then again, consoles don't have to be practical to be cool. In this chapter, you'll find high-style, low-function designs that are incredibly appealing. And there are plenty of options in between those extremes.

You'll find consoles that sit between the front seats, consoles that sit between the rear seats, and consoles that run the full length of a car from front to back, providing serious character and sometimes even enhancing structural rigidity—proof that consoles don't have to provide storage space to be practical. (Note: You'll find overhead consoles in Chapter 7, which covers headliners and floor coverings.)

When it comes to customizing your vehicle's interior, you can build a console entirely from scratch. You can modify the one you've got. Or you can retrofit a late-model console into a vintage vehicle. As always, the options are limitless.

2

2 When you're rethinking the notion of an executive car, as Lincoln did with this Continental concept, you're going to want to include all the comforts of a plush corner office—things like dual laptop tables that stow inside the rear console and a built-in cabinet to house crystal glassware and a drinks dispenser. *Photo courtesy of Lincoln*

3 How hot is the painted lattice over beige leather in this 1937 Lincoln Zephyr? Adams Rod & Custom built the car.

4 Look closely and you'll discover this suede-bedecked console is actually a floating armrest. Eddie's Rod & Custom built this 1950 Merc, better known as *Miss Lead.*

5 Consoles don't always have to go *between* the seats. Luxurious, leather-wrapped outboard consoles in the back of the Becker Automotive Design/STRUT Cadillac Escalade ESV provide storage, cupholders, and tray tables for working in this mobile office. *Photo courtesy of Becker Automotive Design*

3

4

5

6 Want to hide gauges and controls for an Air Ride Technologies suspension? A slick, slide-open console does the trick in *Chocolate Thunder*, the stunning 1937 Ford built by Rad Rides by Troy. *Photo courtesy of Rad Rides by Troy*

7 A painted console really stands out as different in a 1965 Ford Mustang. This clean installation matches the car's exterior paint and provides some contrast with the black-and-white interior.

8 When is a console not really a console? Perhaps when it's part of the body, as it is in this 1932 Ford. Or perhaps it's just a particularly well-integrated console. You be the judge.

9 A simple armrest atop the carpeted trans tunnel is a sufficient console for the 1935 *Aeroliner Sport* open-air roadster built by POSIES. Make no mistake: Subtle can be serious. Note how the stitching down the armrest's center does a beautiful job of echoing the seat stitching, right down to the spacing. *Photo courtesy of POSIES*

10 This 1955 Chevy proves that a late-model center console can look right at home in a vintage ride—and it can provide late-model-style comforts, including a sizable storage compartment and climate control vents for back-seat passengers.

11 More than 300,000 Swarovski crystals adorn the D.A.D. Mercedes-Benz SL600, both inside and out. Plenty of the sparkly little buggers grace the *Million Dollar Car's* waterfall console and shift knob. Smaller crystals even coat the outer edges of the climate-control knobs.

12 Ron Mangus of Hot Rod Interiors is responsible for the inside of this 1934 Ford roadster, which was built by California Custom & Classics. The detailed leather trim flows smoothly across the bottom of the dash and on down the console. Paint and pinstriping tie it all together beautifully, with subtle stripes drawing the eye down the console.

13 Holden created an elegant art deco look for the center console in its Efijy custom coupe concept. The stitched leather, Mother of Pearl, and polished and painted metal look fabulous with the retro pushbutton shifter. *Photo courtesy of Holden*

Dash/Console Combos

Is it a dash or a console? Blending the two can create dramatically different—and dramatically good—looks. Take this 1951 Mercury dash/console combo (left), with its impressive character lines and sweet pinstriping. Or consider the Dodge ZEO concept car (center). Its free-floating, Super White console extends all the way back, and the controls are set flush to achieve a clean, almost skeletal effect. Meanwhile, there's something almost android-like about the BMW Gina Light concept's interior (right). Maybe it's the matte black and brown surfaces offset by brushed stainless. The effect is somehow simple and futuristic at the same time. And don't forget the Nova on the first page of this chapter; its dash/console combo is simply spectacular.

Photo courtesy of Dodge   *Photo courtesy of BMW*

14 The snubbed end of this console feels a bit like the rear fender on a Harley-Davidson Softail. The glossy paint looks way hot in a 1969 Camaro, and it ties in beautifully with the painted roll cage. Fesler also did an outstanding job of carving out minimal openings for the shifter and the line lock switch. *Photo courtesy of Fesler Built*

15 The Dodge Demon concept was imagined as a driver's car, so every feature on the console was set flush with that brushed-aluminum bezel. Why? To avoid blocking the driver's shift arm regardless of seating position. Even the console's storage area is set far back between the seats. *Photo courtesy of Dodge*

16 Swift Kustomz laid a whole lotta blue suede and black alligator-textured leather inside this 2008 Chevy Tahoe. The result looks more than a bit retro, and it totally transforms an otherwise-stock console.

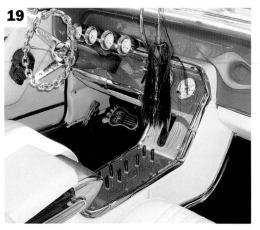

17 You've gotta love contrarians. Sure, plenty of people put Chevy engines in their Fords. But the owner of this car crammed a 514-ci Ford under the hood—and dash and then some—of his 1956 Chevy. The sheetmetal-fabricated console wrapped around the exposed engine pretty much screams, "Forget show! This car was built for go!"

18 Moving most of the controls to the console made it possible to create a smooth, clean dash in this 1941 Willys. Character lines from the dash also flow gracefully into the console.

19 Edog Designs built, painted, and pinstriped this 1966 Ford Thunderbird, with its hand-formed fiberglass dash and custom steel console insert. The cool console trim is factory—an inspired choice to stick with stock.

20 There's not a lot of room for a console in a Deuce, but Pyramid Street Rods built a sweet, subtle space divider to house the B&M shifter. The raised edges make reference to the high/low upholstery throughout this impressive interior. (Gabe's Upholstery did all that leather work in just three weeks.)

21

22

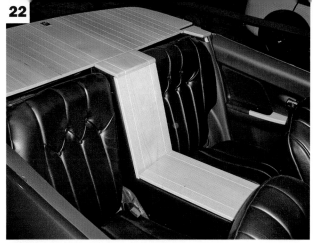

21 Rad Rides by Troy built this 1940 Ford called *Vision*, and Griffin Interiors crafted the stunning inside. The ridged, teardrop-shaped console blends beautifully with the interior's organic points-and-curves motif. The matching teardrop-shaped shift boot—in fabric to match the door panels and seats—is the *pièce de résistance*.

22 A high-end yachting look has been making its way into some notable cars these days. This somewhat more accessible adaptation does a nice job of neatly stowing the convertible top and then carrying the boat-deck theme into the interior.

23 The Jeep Renegade concept has a sort of nonconsole between the seats. It's actually set down into the one-piece molded interior compartment tub. Inside the console, a thermal unit makes it possible to either heat or cool food. *Photo courtesy of Jeep*

24 The Galpin Auto Sports crew went green in a big, bad way with the *Bio Rocket*. This 1965 Chevy Impala not only sports an 800-horsepower biodiesel-powered Duramax engine, its seats and center console are covered in fabric made from 100 percent recycled fibers. *Photo courtesy of Galpin Auto Sports*

23

24

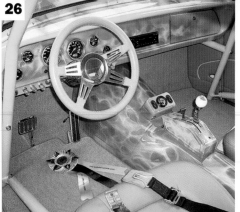

25 A carbon-fiber insert and matching carbon-fiber shift knob add a nice hint of texture atop this stock 1970 Chevrolet Chevelle console. Little changes really can set a car apart.

26 Who says Studebakers aren't hot? This race-ready 1953 boasts a smokin' transmission tunnel that doubles as a sort of center console. It's nice to see the flamed paint job carried through onto the shifter base and the gauge mounting box.

27 The full-length console acts as a central spine in the Jeep Trailhawk concept. The console provides open-bin storage along its entire length, while two enclosed combination storage bins/armrests can move fore and aft along concealed tracks. *Photo courtesy of Jeep*

Kitchen Countertop Materials

Why not let home-improvement options inspire an interior? The center console and shift knob in Lincoln's Mark X two-seat luxury convertible concept (left) are perhaps the finest examples of Corian inside an automobile that I've ever seen—and also perhaps the only ones, if you don't count RVs. The console flows seamlessly into the dash, and it's finished with ribbed dark chrome and natural-grain leather. At the other end of the kitchen counter materials spectrum, the Maybach Landaulet limousine concept (right) features black granite, along with striking Seychelles white leather, "piano-varnish" wood trim, and genuine gold detailing. Its rear console is home to a DVD player, a six-CD changer, and a cooler compartment that holds glasses, goblets, and champagne bottles safely in position.

Photo courtesy of Lincoln

Photo courtesy of Maybach

28 Like a kid wrapping his arm around his test paper, the center console in the Toyota FT-HS concept says, "Mine. Don't look." That titanium-topped ridge is part of the delta-wing driver's pod, which starts at the rear of the console and wraps around the dash. Okay, so the area outside the ridge does provide a bit of an armrest for the front passenger, but still, no peeking. *Photo courtesy of Toyota*

29 The full-length console in Summit Racing's 1961 Ford Starliner sports serious character lines, yards of bone leather, and an awesome arching armrest. Painless Wiring and Air Ride suspension controls are hidden inside. ProRides built the car, and Appleman Interiors is responsible for the seats and all that upholstery.

30 Echoing the twin round gauges with twin round vents in the console is a particularly nice touch inside this 1937 Ford Cabriolet.

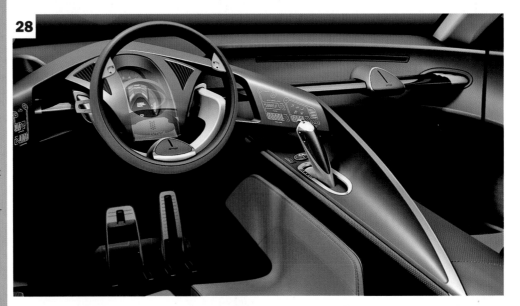

31

32

33

34

35

31 Symmetry is so pleasing, isn't it? It took a great eye to position this many controls and gauges on a console—including the stereo head unit and the Vintage Air controller—yet still leave it feeling neat and tidy.

32 The billet interior theme extends from the dash and steering wheel to the center console in this 1957 Chevy 210. The practical design keeps stereo controls handy and includes a Big Gulp–size cupholder.

33 This white leather-swathed console swells to fill the space between the seats—and provide some storage space—inside a 1960 Ford Starliner.

34 The green-painted stripe on a fiberglass center console beautifully divides the passenger compartment in this 1933 Speedstar, extending all the way up between the seats. Upholstery Unlimited applied plenty of Saddle distressed leather as well. *Photo courtesy of Upholstery Unlimited*

35 Ford's F-250 Super Chief concept pickup boasts an unusually elegant, manly interior reminiscent of an old-school gentleman's club. It's finished in American walnut, brushed aluminum, and rich brown leather, and the trick slide-out rear console has been custom-fitted with crystal glasses, decanters, and ashtrays. *Photo courtesy of Ford*

36 This floating center console runs the entire length of the Ford Forty-Nine concept car's interior. And it's not just for looks; it also stiffens the car's structure. The scale and openness of that shifter mechanism feel almost extravagant these days. *Photo courtesy of Ford*

37 *Popular Hot Rodding* has been working on *Project X*—the same '57 Chevy that starred in the movie *Hollywood Knights*—for more than 40 years now, and the magazine tapped GM Performance Division to completely rebuild the car in 2007. The interior now boasts a widened 1964 Impala console. The unique X logo (as in *Project X*) adorns billet aluminum inserts on the console and dash and outside on the Bel Air trim panels, too.

38 Street Concepts replaced the stock woodgrain edge trim and the stock brushed-metal top insert on this Hyundai Azera console with gloss-black wood, unifying the styling for a classy feel. Amazing how much of a statement you can make with a couple relatively small changes. *Photo courtesy of Street Concepts*

39 Structure, styling statement, and console all in one. It's easy to see why this 1932 Ford roadster built by Hollywood Hot Rods helped shop owner Troy Ladd win the Goodguys 2007 Trendsetter Award. Check out how the curves of the console match the tubular structure of the seats, and how the console's striking circular cutouts match the seat stitching.

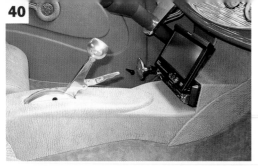

40 Upholstery Unlimited laid a whole lot of adobe-colored Sedona Nubuck leather on the console in this 1933 Speedstar. The console's sensuous shapes go beautifully with the door panels, not to mention with the car's sexy body. *Photo courtesy of Upholstery Unlimited*

41 *Ice Cold* (a Chevy pickup) boasts a painted console to match its exterior. Do you suppose anybody would actually attempt to sit on that little pad, or is it just a snazzy armrest?

42 Panoz Auto Development built this McDreamy 1965 Mustang for actor Patrick Dempsey (from the TV show *Grey's Anatomy*). The redesigned console features a wealth of materials—leather, suede, carpet, and polished metals—that are consistent throughout the interior. Somehow, it manages to look both retro and high-tech, which is an overriding theme for this resto mod.

43 Circles are a recurring design theme inside this 1954 Ford Victoria, including the cutouts on the console trim, the vents, the shift knob, and the cutouts on the shifter handle and mounting plate. Kaucher Kustoms designed the car, and Downtown Willy crafted the interior.

44 When you think *luxury* and *Lincoln Navigator* in the same sentence, you definitely think champagne, right? Hence, the dual champagne bottle holders that are motorized to raise and lower in the rear console of the *Navigator LUX*, built by Galpin Auto Sports. *Photo courtesy of Galpin Auto Sports*

45 Man, is that painted console pretty. The way it picks up the contours of the dash is inspiring, and so is the way its rear end is stitched into the leather. Fesler built this 1969 Chevy Blazer. *Photo courtesy of Fesler Built*

46 Extruded aluminum beams tie the dashboard into the console in the Dodge Razor concept, providing a strong architectural, yet racing-inspired look. Simple body-color metal cutouts continue the integration between dash and console and hide any necessary wiring. *Photo courtesy of Dodge*

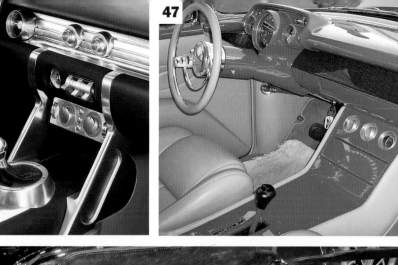

47 A pop-open storage compartment in the console mimics a pop-open compartment right above it in the dash of this 1957 Chevy Nomad. Together, they provide a really clean look. Placing the climate-control vents in the console also cleans up the dash, and the choice of infinitely adjustable porthole-style vents makes it easy to keep driver and passengers comfortable.

48 Would you believe this is a 1962 Impala SS? Actually, the dash is original under that custom airbrushing, but the center console is completely hand-crafted. And my, what a large center console it is. It's clad in black leather to match the seats, which feature real ostrich-skin inserts.

49 See that basic-looking monitor? It actually can show two different movies at the same time, one angled toward each rear-seat passenger in the Chrysler Imperial concept. All of the entertainment system controls are beautifully installed on the console, along with rear-zone climate controls and buttons to activate rear-seat heaters. *Photo courtesy of Chrysler*

Chapter 6
Hardware

Hardware may not sound like a sexy topic, but swapping something as simple as the steering wheel can have a profound impact on a vehicle's style. You can make a dramatic difference with other little changes, too, such as switching out the knobs on the dash or changing the shift knob.

In this chapter, you'll find a fun assortment of needful things, including all of the above, plus pedals and door handles, necker knobs and window cranks, rearview mirrors and shifters, too.

1 From the chain steering wheel to the extralong shift lever topped with a hand holding a purple skull, this Ford certainly has some attention-getting hardware. Edog Designs built the 1966 Thunderbird. The slick purple switches for the windows and air suspension were purchased at a truck stop; they're actually made for big rigs. *Photo courtesy of Edog Designs*

2 The Chrysler ecoVoyager concept was designed to be on par with a private jet, so it's no surprise to find individual armrests up front with window controls and seat heat and massage switches built right in. *Photo courtesy of Chrysler*

3 Have you ever seen a better-looking rearview mirror? POSIES crafted this stunning art deco piece for the 1935 *Aeroliner*. It makes me want to look at high-end bathroom faucets and towel hooks for more inspiration. *Photo courtesy of POSIES*

4 Controls for the Vintage Air system, the power windows, and more are neatly hidden inside the stunning console in this 1932 Ford three-window coupe, which took home Goodguys' 2008 award for America's Most Beautiful Street Rod.

5 You know the folks at Classic Design Concepts have a sense of humor when they outfit their 1967 Ford Mustang Flashback concept with an eject button. The question is: Does it eject the driver or the front passenger?

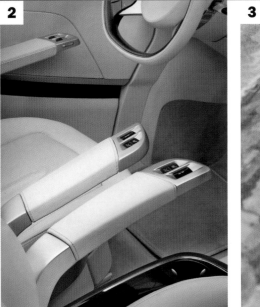

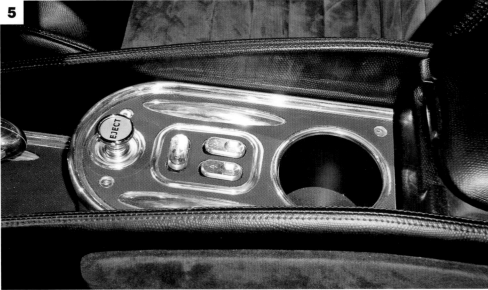

6

7

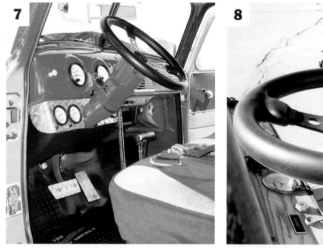

8

9

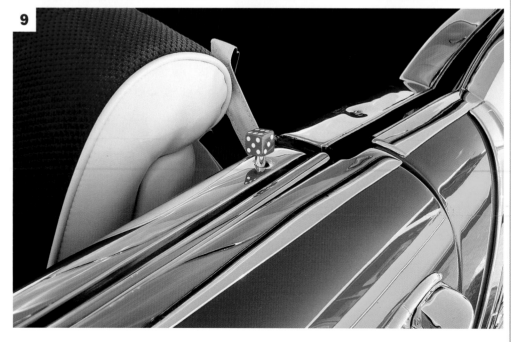

6 A woodgrain rim that matches the shift knob really sets off the six-spoke wheel in this 1930 Ford Model A.

7 Diamond-plate pedals match the dash trim and look particularly manly in this 1949 Chevy truck.

8 Okay, so a necker knob (a.k.a. suicide knob or Brodie knob) is an old-school idea, but a skull does make it more *au courant*. The skull design is particularly appropriate in this 1923 Ford C-Cab called *Grim Reaper's Coach.*

9 You hardly see regular old door locks anymore, what with the preponderance of poppers. But these dice do have a fun, retro feel.

10 The laminated knobs on the dash and the laminated shift knob really play up the red, white, and black theme in this 1928 Ford.

11 The Ford SYNUS concept has a soft-touch steering wheel covered—and partially filled—with memory foam. Also check out the nifty, one-off pedals. *Photo courtesy of Ford*

12 The pedals—and the finger grooves in the shift knob—work well with the rhythm set by all that brightwork on the dash in *Ruby Begonia*, a 1951 Merc that's the mascot of Galvin Precision Machining.

13 Fesler installed paddle shifters behind the pleasing dual-three-spoke steering wheel in this radically modified 1969 Chevy Blazer. *Photo courtesy of Fesler Built*

14 Okay, so it doesn't *do* anything, but this skull detail on the package shelf of a 1954 Chevy Bel Air sure looks cool.

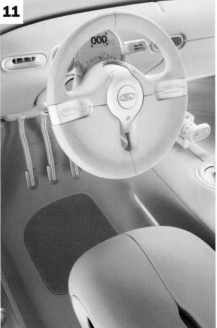

Shift Knobs

Skulls. Tikis. Beer bottles. Hand grenades. Eight balls. Pistons. If you're looking to express your inner self, look no further than the shift knob. It doesn't matter if you've got a floor shifter or a column shifter, you can find off-the-shelf options to make you smile every time you get into your car—or you can craft a truly custom piece.

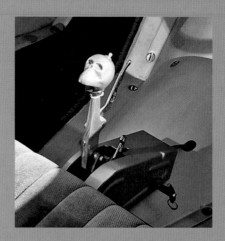

Photo courtesy of CarSponsorships.com

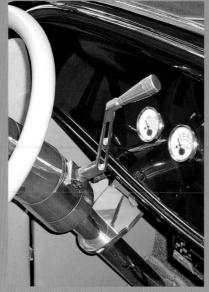

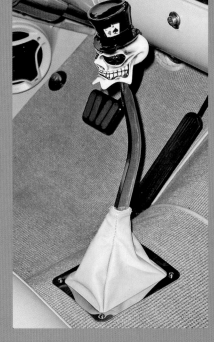

Photo courtesy of Upholstery Unlimited

Shifters

Shift knobs certainly aren't the only gear-selection components to consider. Of course, choosing the right shifter goes far beyond style; a shifter is a key performance part. But it also can be stunning, as demonstrated (from left) by POSIES in its art deco 1935 *Aeroliner* and by the handmade piece in *Mercules,* a 1950 Mercury. Installation is everything, too. For instance, Upholstery Unlimited crafted a console with an opening that precisely accommodates the range of motion of a B&M shifter (far right).

Photo courtesy of POSIES　　　　　　　　　　　　　　　　　*Photo courtesy of Upholstery Unlimited*

15 There's not a lot of legroom in a 1923 Ford T-bucket, so this one sports an angled brake pedal for left foot stopping.

16 What could be better for a woody than a wood-framed mirror in the shape of a surfboard? *Monster Garage* built this 1950 Ford, a.k.a. the *Ultimate Surfmobile.*

17 Neatly hidden behind the seat back: The handle on the driver side is the trunk release, while the other lever is a battery disconnect in this 1933 Ford roadster with an interior by Upholstery Unlimited. *Photo courtesy of Upholstery Unlimited*

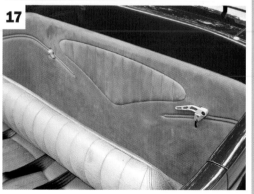

18 This 1950 Ford sports some fun hardware, from the necker knob that matches the fuzzy dice to the piston shift knob, not to mention the knobs on the dash.

19 Whether you've got a seriously chopped top or a big visor out front, you're gonna need a prism to see the stoplights. Heck, even if you don't need a prism, it looks cool and it's a great conversation piece.

20 It's hardware heaven in this 1965 Ford Mustang fastback, with the cool pedals, the wrench-turned-emergency-brake-handle, and even a ratchet as a turn signal stalk.

21 Have you noticed that rat rodders like really long shift levers? This one definitely reached its limit.

Pedals

Do you want big pedals or petite ones? Off-the-shelf or custom? Flamed? Logo'ed? With or without a dead pedal? You've got plenty of choices. You can even play up the mechanicals that connect the pedals . . . or not.

Photo courtesy of Honda

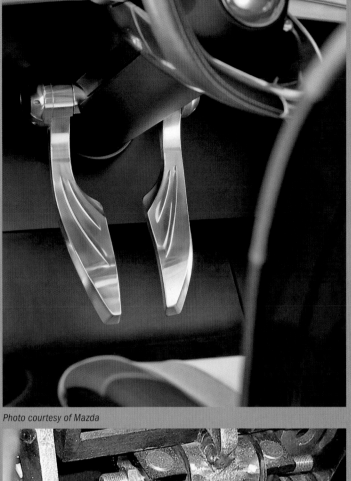

Photo courtesy of Mazda

Photo courtesy of Toyota

Steering Wheels

Perhaps the dominant piece of hardware in any interior is the steering wheel. It's the first thing you notice in most rides, and it's certainly the part you'll be closest to in your own. These days, you can buy off-the-shelf steering wheels in an almost dizzying assortment of styles, from retro to modern, from leather-wrapped to textured, from polished wood to painted. Chain wheels have even made a comeback. Plus, manufacturers are offering a broad range of sizes and spoke styles, not to mention spoke quantities. And, again, there's always the full-custom approach.

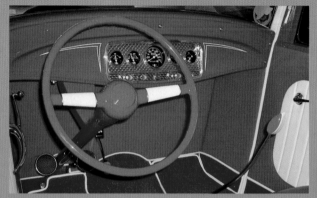

Photo courtesy of Upholstery Unlimited

Photos courtesy of Grant Products

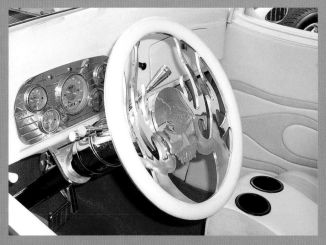 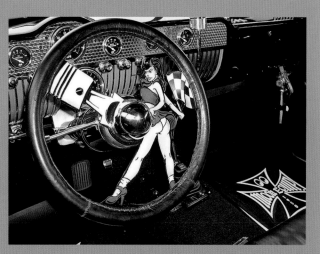

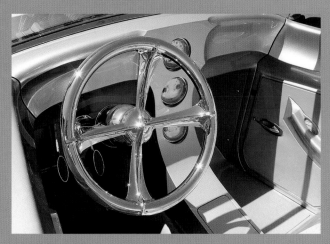 

Photo by Jody Wetherill

Door Handles and Window Cranks

Shiny. Matte. Painted. Door handles and window pulls come in a variety of styles, or you can make your own. And then there's the installation. You can position these pieces so they're a focal point, or you can make them more subtle. You can mount them up high or down low on the doors. You can install a discreet door release behind the doors, or you can position these controls on the center console.

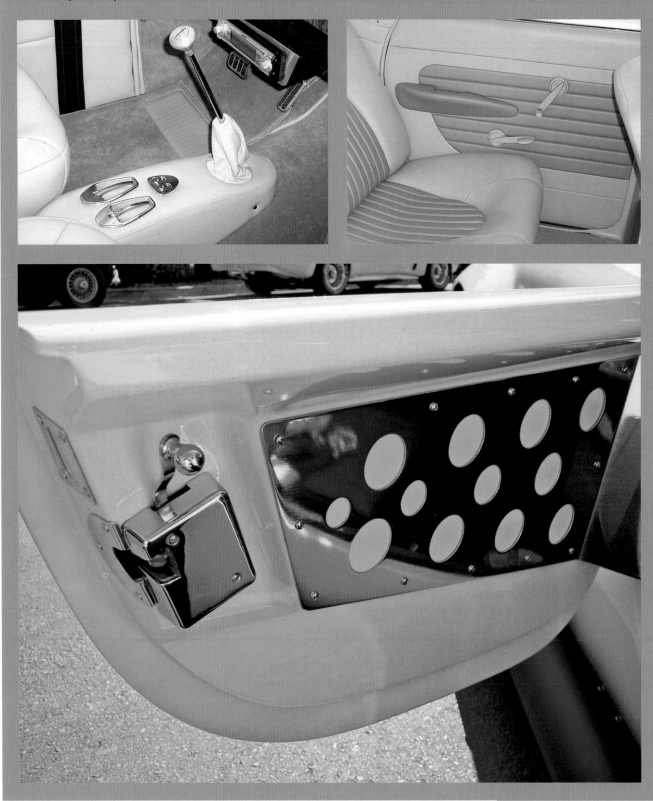

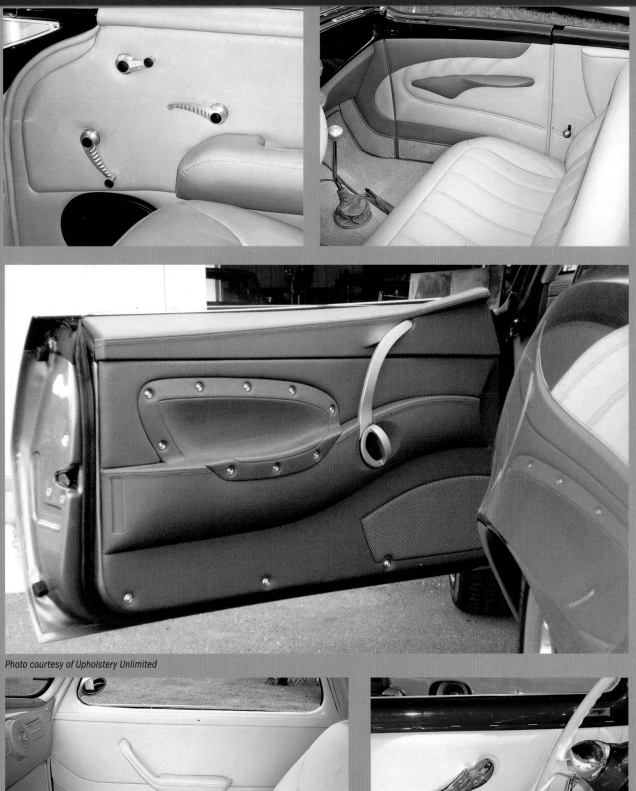

Photo courtesy of Upholstery Unlimited

Chapter 7
Floor Coverings and Headliners

Look up. Look down. When it comes to covering the floor and ceiling of your ride, there are considerably more possibilities than most people can imagine, let alone name. Carpet, metal, leather, suede, cloth, paint—the possibilities are limited only by your imagination, and potentially, your budget. For many people, practicality clearly is not a concern.

2 Again, it may not be the most practical choice, but thick white carpet looks luxurious in this 1941 Willys, which won Best Interior at the Grand Sierra Resort during Hot August Nights 2008 and was a runner-up for Goodguys' 2008 America's Most Beautiful Street Rod award.

3 Believe it or not, those are rubber floor mats. But, man, do they look stunning inside the 1932 Ford sedan delivery built by FastLane Rod Shop. It was named Goodguys' 2008 Street Rod of the Year.

4 The semi-gloss floor material in Ford's Model U concept runs all the way from the top of the instrument panel up over the fuel cell–powered SUV's hydrogen storage tanks and on back to the tailgate. Three slots allow components to be mounted wherever it's convenient, and they also provide power. *Photo courtesy of Ford*

5 Perforated metal mezzanine-style flooring pays homage to the industrial history of Detroit—and looks absolutely striking—in the Chrysler SR 392 Roadster. Just don't drop anything small while you're driving.

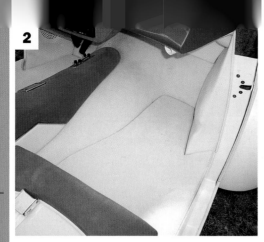

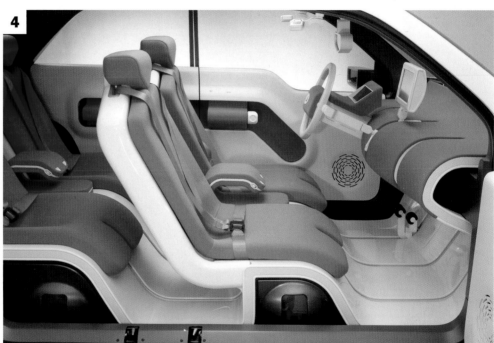

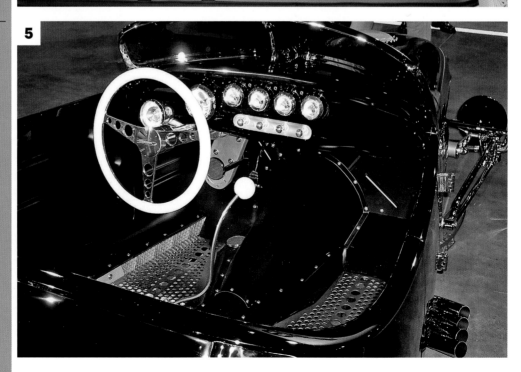

6 A machined metal kickplate matches the door detailing inside this 1965 Cobra, and it really stands out against the plain black carpet.

7 A combination of wood paneling and carpet makes for a standout floor in this open-top 1930 Model A Ford.

8 Camouflage-patterned sheet metal on the rear floor of the Hummer HX concept gives a lighthearted nod to more hardworking Humvees. *Photo courtesy of Hummer*

Traditional Street Rod Styling

Want a really traditional street rod look? Opt for carpet with contrasting trim (usually leather) that emphasizes the contours of your floorboards, as in a 1953 Chevy pickup (left) and a 1932 Ford highboy.

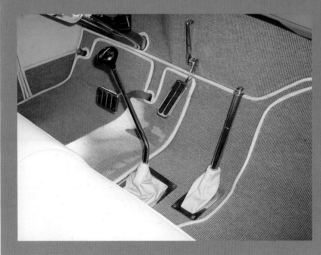

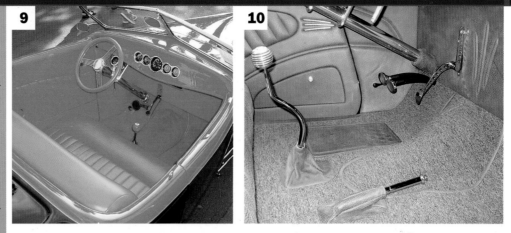

9 Plush red carpet contributes to the monochromatic look that is so pleasing inside this 1932 Ford.

10 A leather footrest inset within the carpet matches the leather on the firewall and the door panels in this 1933 Ford roadster, with an interior by Upholstery Unlimited. *Photo courtesy of Upholstery Unlimited*

Naked Floors

Bare metal certainly has that bare-essentials quality. Consider the impeccably formed sheet metal in this Shadow Rods lengthened 1927 Ford roadster (top left), the visible welds in the Skoty Chops Kustoms rat rod (top right), the industrial-strength diamond plate in this Gasser-style Willys (bottom left), and the barely there diamond plate in this 1931 open-top (and partly open-bottom) coupe.

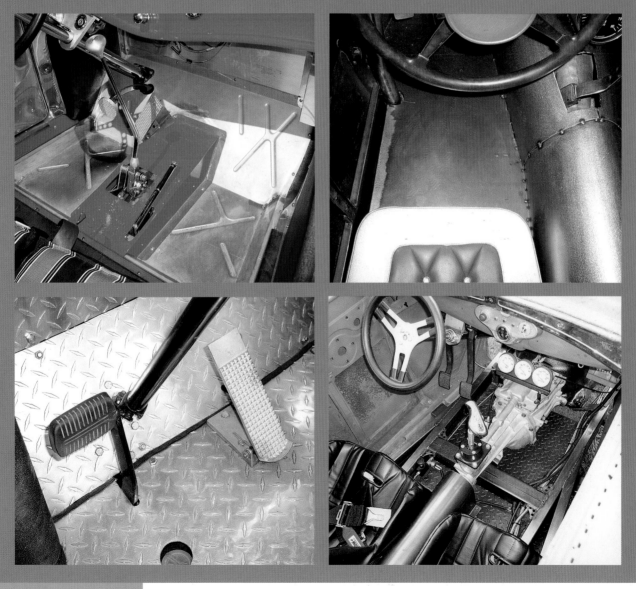

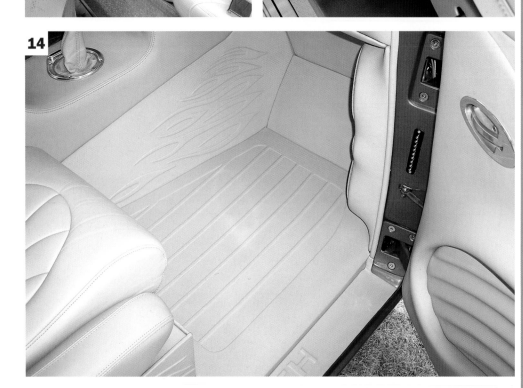

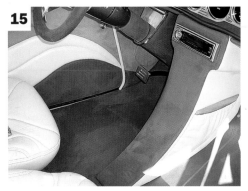

11 Rubber? You bet. The Jeep Compass concept features a molded rubber floor that's as stunning as it is easy to hose clean. *Photo courtesy of Jeep*

12 The Ford Explorer Sportsman concept was designed with fly fishing enthusiasts in mind, and it sports exceptionally cool bloodwood floor mats. The beautiful wood is found in coastal forests in Australia. *Photo courtesy of Ford*

13 Even carpet and floor mats manage to look exciting inside the 1950 Mercury known as *Wasabi*, thanks to the fun green color and the glittery silver-metallic threads.

14 Jon Lind Interiors finished the insides of the *Waza '49* Plymouth with $24,000 worth of leather, including this strikingly embossed floor.

15 This 1934 Plymouth sedan is swaddled in suede—even the floor. Now that's got to feel nice on bare feet.

16 This 1932 Ford roadster sports another great leather floor look, with contoured detailing to match the door panels.

17 Red and white checkered paint looks fun and vaguely reminiscent of the tablecloths in old-school Italian restaurants, and it's certainly perfect for this over-the-top 1960 VW Bug.

18 Alabaster leather floor covering features orange alligator-embossed trim to match the seats in this 1948 Chevrolet Blazer, a.k.a. *Impression.* The extremely professional build was handled by the truck's owner, 21-year-old Robbie Acevedo, who's opened his own shop called Pacific Coast Customs.

19 An aluminum footrest for the passenger matches the aluminum pedals and footrest on the driver side in the Audi TT Clubsport Quattro concept. *Photo courtesy of Audi*

20 Ford's Forty-Nine concept pays homage to the 1949 Ford, the first all-new postwar design—a car so well received that it won the prestigious Fashion Academy Award. This iteration definitely features high-fashion flooring: silver carpet with chrome rails that run all the way from front to rear. *Photo courtesy of Ford*

21 Spray-on bedliner provides a nonskid, easy-to-clean surface inside this 1947 Willys CJ2A jeep that's clearly built for off-roading.

22 It would be a shame to cover up these mind-bogglingly beautiful welds, but a touch of carpet does add some plushness—and protection—to the floor of this 1966 Chevy II race car.

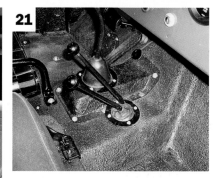

105

Floor Mats

Floor mats can make a styling statement quickly, easily, and inexpensively. And clearly they're available in a huge assortment of styles, including (clockwise from top) leopard and camouflage patterns from GG Bailey; Coco Auto Mats made from coconut fiber, Diamond Plate AutoMats, and Leather AutoMats from Intro-Tech Automotive; and fun rubber skull mats from Plasticolor.

Photo courtesy of GG Bailey

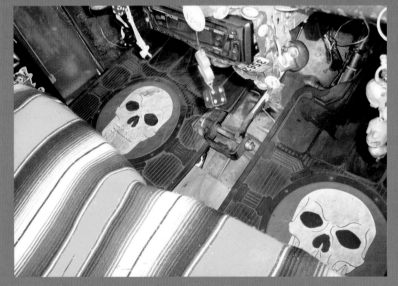

Photo courtesy of GG Bailey

Photo courtesy of Intro-Tech Automotive

Photo courtesy of Intro-Tech Automotive

Photo courtesy of Intro-Tech Automotive

23 The glass roof of Ford's Super Chief concept features a leather-wrapped grid of American walnut. If you were to peer down through that roof, you'd see a continuous expanse of walnut flooring outlined in aluminum; it extends through the cabin and into the pickup's bed. *Photo courtesy of Ford*

Headliners

24 Galpin Auto Sports' *Bio Rocket* 1965 Chevy Impala features a headliner made from 100 percent recycled fibers—proof that going green can still be high style. *Photo courtesy of Galpin Auto Sports*

25 The Ford SYNUS concept actually features memory foam for the headliner and side panels. The whole idea was to provide a warm, inviting interior that's a fun oasis within a sometimes-cruel urban environment. *Photo courtesy of Ford*

26 Long popular as seat coverings, Mexican blankets clearly work as a headliner material, too. Purple skulls are a recurring theme in this 1966 Ford Thunderbird built by Edog Designs. *Photo courtesy of Edog Designs*

23

24

25 **26**

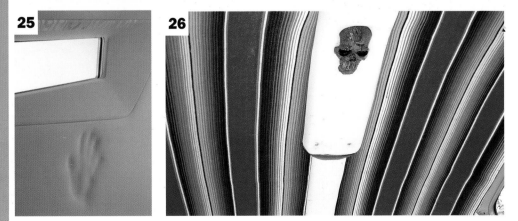

The headliner in the Holden Efijy concept feels like a stock 1950s-style approach, but a closer look reveals it's not fabric. It's actually leather. *Photo courtesy of Holden*

Wood Ceilings

Wood looks good for a ceiling in a home, but it might look even better as a headliner for a hot rod. Check out (clockwise from top left) the maple inside this 1937 Chevy woody, the maple with painted steel filler panels in the 1932 Ford sedan delivery built by FastLane Rod Shop, and both the cab and cargo area in a 1923 Ford C-Cab dubbed the *Grim Reaper's Coach*.

Lengthwise

You normally see stripes running from side to side for a headliner, but lengthwise stripes really emphasize the long lines in a ride.

Side to Side

Now here's the more traditional headliner approach with stripes running from side to side. Chromed factory ribs and custom velour exude class in a 1955 Chevy Bel Air (left), while body-color piped stripes dress up the long expanse of headliner in a 1955 Chevy sedan delivery.

Sunvisors

Sunvisors certainly don't have to be anything elaborate. Apply a little upholstery to match the headliner, perhaps some piping to finish off the edges, and you're good to go, as in this 1955 Chevy Nomad (with interior by Armand's Auto Upholstery). Of course, there are ways to have fun, even with something as mundane as a visor. Take the vintage license plates used in Stone's Speed & Sport's 1940 Ford pickup.

Color, Pattern, and Texture

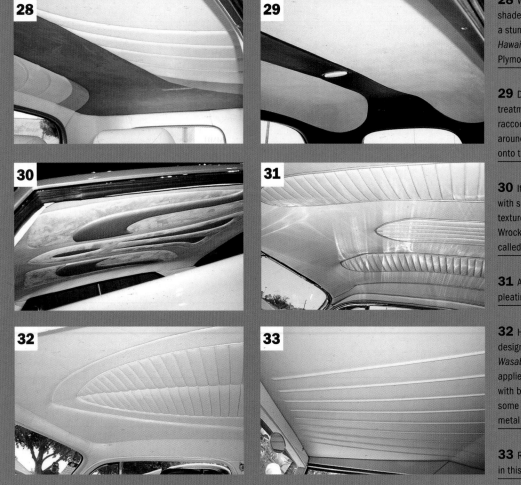

28 White leather and two shades of suede make for a stunning headliner in the *Hawaiian Orchid* 1934 Plymouth sedan.

29 Does this headliner treatment remind you of a raccoon? The black wraps nicely around the windows and down onto the sail panels and A-pillars.

30 It's deluxe and delicious—with suede and smooth and textured leather—inside the Wrocket Products–built Chevy called *Killer 67 Nova-Star*.

31 A lot of piping, a lot of pleating, a lot of style.

32 Hi-Speed Rods & Customs designed the 1950 Merc called *Wasabi*, and Eddie Salcido applied all that white leather with beautiful stitching, including some leather with a hammered-metal texture.

33 Ribbed can look so right, as in this 1933 Ford.

34 Cowabunga, baby! *Monster Garage* transformed a rusted-out 1950 Ford wagon into the *Ultimate Surfmobile*, complete with this fun fabric headliner.

35 I think it could be a Chevy. The metal trim around the Bowtie adds some great texture.

36 The flat panorama-style roof of Scion's Hako concept doesn't have a headliner, *per se*. Instead, it has a random barcode-like pattern that's visible both inside and out. Now that's different. *Photo courtesy of Scion*

37 Covering every surface inside this 1936 Studebaker Dictator with burgundy velour creates a serious bordello look.

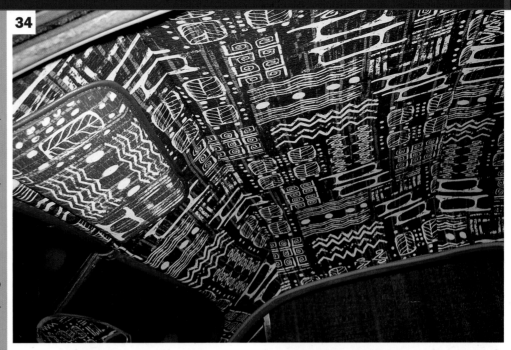

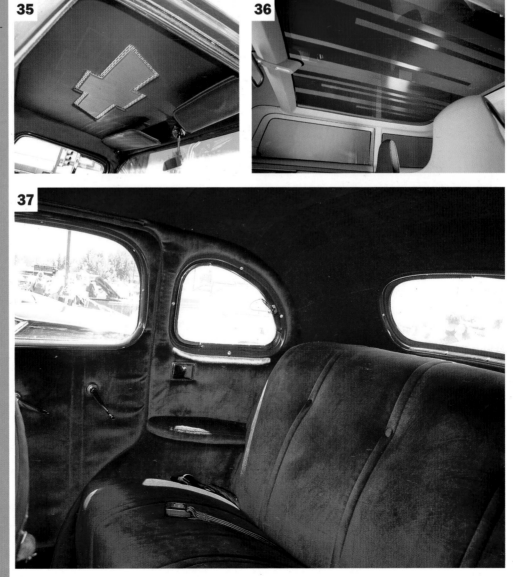

38

39

40

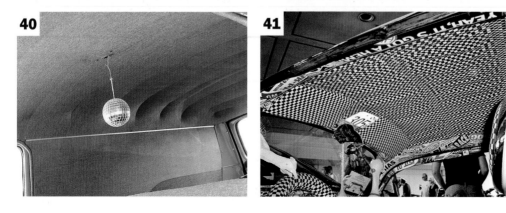

41

38 A molded headliner with flames looks sweet in suede in this home-built 1948 Chevy truck.

39 Galpin Auto Sports' biodiesel/hydrogen-powered Ford F-450 Super Duty pickup, called *BioHydro*, actually boasts a headliner made of hemp from Enviro Textiles and a carpet made from recycled plastic soda bottles. *Photo courtesy of Galpin Auto Sports*

40 Nothing says "party barge" quite like a disco ball! Don't you want to dance the night away inside this 1954 Ford Courier?

41 We'll have fun, fun, fun until somebody takes this 1960 VW Beetle away.

Overhead Consoles

Storage space in a car is like closets in a house—you can never have too much or too many. And a great way to stash stuff out of the way is to take a cue from new vehicles: add an overhead console, like (clockwise from top left) the stunning ostrich-trimmed unit in this 1938 Chevy pickup, the pretty body color–painted console in this 1939 Chevy coupe, or the nicely matched two-tone multi-compartment model in this 1941 Chevy coupe.

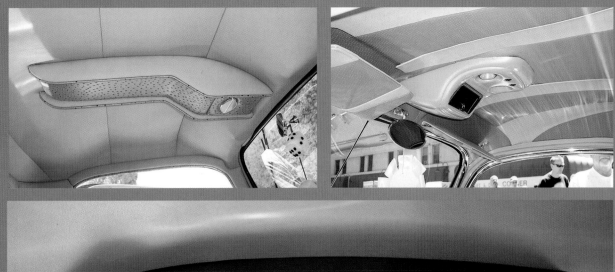

42 It's amazing how fabulous perforated leather can look, as it most certainly does in the POSIES-built 1929 Ford pickup called *ThunderRoad. Photo courtesy of POSIES*

113

Dome Lights

Even something as simple as a dome light provides plenty of room for self-expression, with all the different styles and different mounting locations. You might even consider installing a second light for back-seat passengers.

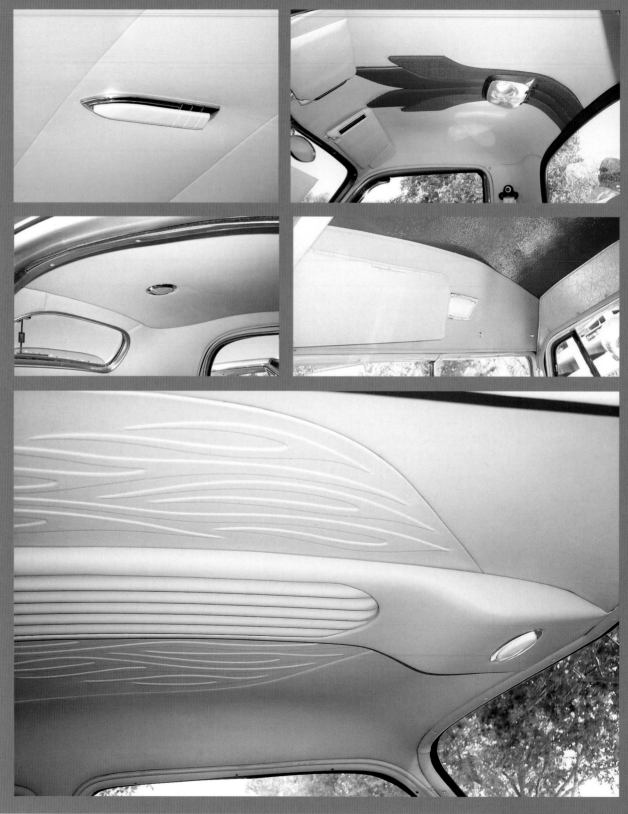

43 Pinstripe-style stitching sets this headliner apart, as do bands of red for contrast between the vehicle's different areas—one at the windshield, one behind the seats, and another at the rear.

1 The trunk in this 1957 Buick Special looks comfortable enough to be a couch. It even has a good-size storage compartment under the floor.

Chapter 8
Trunks and Cargo Areas

Trunks and cargo areas are among the most practical parts of an interior. After all, they were designed as storage space—closets for an automobile, so to speak.

But, of course, not everybody believes in being practical. So you'll see the full gamut of trunk and cargo area treatments here, from spaces that are filled with equipment to wide-open, usable areas.

You'll find the full gamut of materials, too, from bare metal to plush upholstery, and from leather and carpet to rubber, all done up in a remarkable and delightful variety of tastes and styles.

And then, for even more ideas on how to fill up a trunk or cargo area, be sure to check out the next chapter on audio and high-tech accessories.

2 Three Crowns Speed & Kustoms built the *Imperial Roadster*, a 1931 Ford that features new-old-stock (NOS) 1959 DeSoto vinyl and NOS 1957 Chrysler Imperial fabric throughout its interior.

3 Upholstery Unlimited crafted the stunning trunk of *Razor*, a 1969 Chevrolet Camaro built by Ringbrothers, that won Goodguys' 2008 Street Machine of the Year award. Remove a couple fasteners here or there, and you gain quick access to the battery, amplifiers, and other hidden goodies. *Photo courtesy of Upholstery Unlimited*

4 There's not a lot of room in the trunk of this Deuce, but allowing the compartment to have some funky contours and drop down as low as possible provides space for a couple of overnight bags at least.

5 Can you see why this 1932 Ford three-window coupe won Goodguys' award for America's Most Beautiful Street Rod in 2008? All-Ways Hot Rods built *My Girl*, and Lux Interiors crafted a truly luxe trunk with striking brightwork and incredible attention to detail.

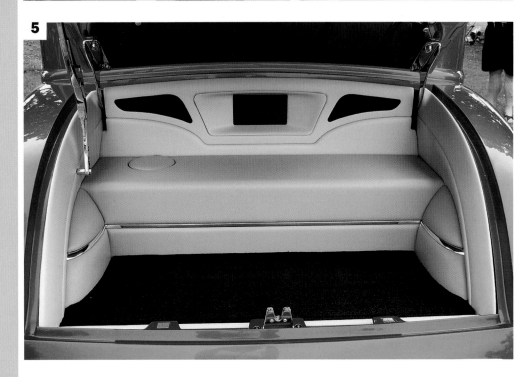

Fitted Luggage

There's something particularly luxurious and "old money" about fitted luggage. In the case of the Lincoln Continental concept (top), you just hit a button on the remote and a large tray slides out of the trunk, offering access to Zero Halliburton luggage and golf club cases. For a beautifully integrated look, Upholstery Unlimited crafted a pair of leather-wrapped bags to fit the trunk of this 1933 Ford. As you can see, they're not exactly a standard suitcase shape.

Photo courtesy of Lincoln

Photo courtesy of Upholstery Unlimited

Photo courtesy of Upholstery Unlimited

6

7

8

6 Eddie Salcido created the stunning white leather trunk for *Wasabi*, a 1950 Mercury that boasts metallic carpet to match its PPG paint.

7 Don't know about you, but I'd be afraid of spilling gas in the clean carpeted and upholstered trunk of this 1941 Willys.

8 Painted or powdercoated metal can look really striking in a trunk—and it's a cool way to show off beautiful metal fabrication work, as in this 1940 Ford.

9 Providing a nice combination of practicality and fun, the trunk in this 1947 Ford three-window coupe includes tool storage, a handy jack, and a pair of monitors for a little audiovisual entertainment.

10 Traditional tuck and roll and mirrored tiles make a plush statement in this 1964 Buick Riviera, crafted by low rider legend Bob Mercado and featured on the TV show *Livin' the Low Life*. *Photo by Jennifer Shields, courtesy of BCII/Livin' the Low Life*

9

10

Trunk Lids

There's nothing *wrong* with a painted trunk lid, of course, but there's something *so right* about upholstery in this unexpected, extra-credit area. Add a little sound-deadening material and you score a quieter ride, too. Cases in point, from left: a 1956 Chevy Bel Air, a 1939 Chevy coupe, and the 1967 Chevy Nova-Star (interior by Wrocket Products).

11

11 This unbelievably fun 1960 Volkswagen Beetle takes custom to a whole 'nother level. Of course, since the engine resides in the rear, the trunk is up front, complete with a no-longer-usable spare tire and a crafty storage compartment.

12 HiTek Hot Rods built this red, red, red 1960 Chevrolet Corvette, which features a beautifully detailed leather-and-carpet trunk.

13 Dove gray carpet and leather give the trunk of this 1933 Ford a soft and upscale look.

12

13

14 Cimtex Rods built this 1957 Olds Fiesta wagon, which has a trick sheetmetal housing for the Air Ride Technologies suspension equipment. Drop the lid, and the carpeted cargo area has a flat floor for easy loading.

Tool Time

It's always smart to keep tools handy—and even smarter when they fit neatly into a cool tool-storage compartment, as they do in these three very different designs. The 1955 Chevy (left) sports a trio of flush-fit storage areas along the perimeter of its trunk; finger-size notches make them easy to open. Tools tuck up against the lid of the *Cannon Special* 1932 Ford highboy's beautifully detailed trunk (right top), thanks to Santana Interior Designs. And this tidy tool storage compartment is actually hidden beneath that set of custom-fitted luggage in this 1933 Ford roadster trunk crafted by Upholstery Unlimited.

Photo courtesy of Upholstery Unlimited

15

16

17

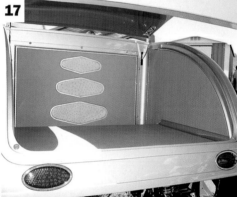

18

19

15 The two-tone paint scheme carries over nicely into the trunk of this 1934 Chevy cabriolet.

16 A simple rubber mat and body-color paint finish off the trunk of *Project X*, the 1957 Chevy 210 that *Popular Hot Rodding* magazine has been building and rebuilding since 1965.

17 Scott's Hotrods 'n' Customs built this 1932 Ford, which sports more leather in its trunk than it does in its almost entirely painted interior. The triple ostrich detailing mimics the minimalist seat upholstery.

18 In honor of the 75th anniversary of the Deuce, Detroit Street Rods crafted a limited edition of 100 1932 Fords based on the Dearborn Deuce convertible. Each wears the official Ford anniversary logo, including one inside the beautifully upholstered trunk.

19 Carpet, smooth leather, and darker perforated leather make for an attention-getting trunk treatment in this 1939 Chevy coupe.

20

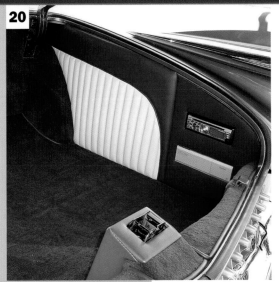

21

20 This 1959 Cadillac Coupe DeVille is deliciously slathered in purple, inside and out. The good-size trunk also provides a convenient space to stash a CD changer and head unit.

21 For cars that really get driven, a spare tire is a necessity of life. Of course, it also can be dirty. A spare tire cover—like the two-tone number in this 1958 Oldsmobile Super 88—can preserve a pristine trunk and protect whatever else you store back there.

22 Sometimes the practical pieces really set a car apart, such as the polished hinges and trunk lid support on this 1937 Ford coupe. A trunk light comes in handy, too.

23 What do you do with the awkward, curved spaces over a set of big wheel tubs? How about turning them into storage compartments, as in this 1955 Chevy 210?

24 Shiny! That's definitely the word for the impeccably hand-formed sheet metal that lines the trunk of this 1965 Cobra.

22

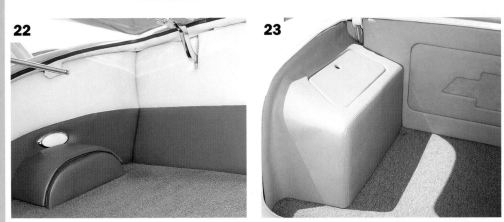

23

24

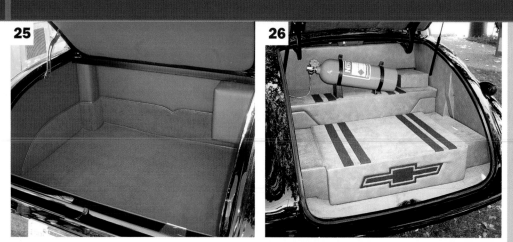

25 Wrapping the carpet partway up the sides of this Deuce trunk provides a nice textural contrast and some really pleasing detailing.

26 A multi-tier approach makes the most of the storage space inside this 1939 Chevy coupe.

Gas 'n' Go

The trunk is certainly a logical place to stash a gas tank or a fuel cell. But making the space functional and spill-proof doesn't have to preclude it from looking good, as demonstrated by (clockwise from top left) a race-ready 1953 Studebaker, a 1932 Ford roadster rat rod, a thirsty 572-ci, 850-horsepower 1968 Plymouth Barracuda, and a Hemi-powered Deuce built by Pyramid Street Rods.

Cargo Areas

27 The striking cargo compartment houses a compressor and controller for the air suspension in this slammed-to-the-ground 1948 Chevy sedan delivery, a.k.a. *One Bad Apple*. The painted panels on the inside walls match the exterior graphics.

28 The design team envisioned the Lincoln MKT concept as a "Learjet of the road," and these nifty rails are not just stylish, they're also practical. A power lift system lets you raise each one individually to help corral cargo, or you can set them all down flush for unrestricted access and space. *Photo courtesy of Lincoln*

29 Carpeting and a tonneau cover turn the bed of a 1991 Chevy Silverado pickup into a giant trunk. T. J. Pagano pinstriped the Bowtie, as well as the truck's interior and body.

30 A carpeted floor with contrasting trim, two trap-door storage compartments, a subtle audio installation, and a headliner treatment that wraps all the way around both sides makes for a clean, attractive, and still incredibly utilitarian cargo area in this 1941 GMC sedan delivery.

31 Vintage drive-in speakers and pinstripe-style stitching add gobs of style to the rear of this '29 Ford Tudor that somehow manages to be both old school and radical.

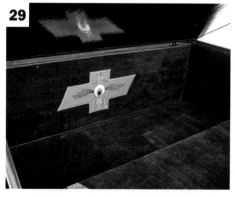

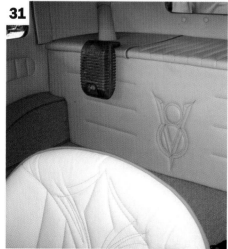

Wood Is Always Good

Wood looks good on the floor of this 1940 Ford sedan delivery's cargo area (left). But proving the theory that more is better, wood looks fantastic when it's used to panel a sedan delivery's *entire* cargo area, as in this 1932 Ford, which was named Goodguys' 2008 Street Rod of the Year.

32 The bed of this 1959 Chevy El Camino has been treated to an ultra-interior-like treatment—complete with sofa-style seating and a drink table—thanks to Max's Upholstery. You may have seen this car on *Livin' the Low Life*. Photo by *Jennifer Shields, courtesy of BCII/ Livin' the Low Life*

33 A wooden platform makes loading cargo easy in this 1941 Chevy Master Deluxe. It's also hinged toward the front, so smaller items can be tucked underneath.

34 Carrying the look of the high-style headliner down and around the sides of the cargo area provides a really pleasing, unified look in this 1937 Ford sedan delivery. Finish Line Automotive Interiors laid down all those yards of two-tone leather.

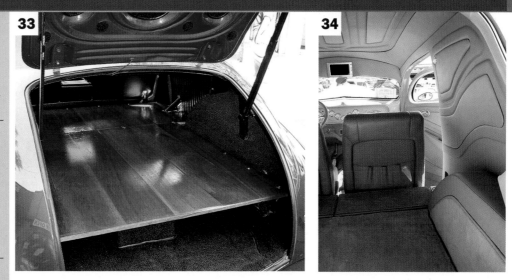

Pull-Out Access

Why not make access easy? In Faurecia's Premium Attitude concept car (top left), the trunk floor and rear bumper lip slide out, creating an easy-access trunk drawer. The Jeep Trailhawk concept (top right) has a sliding Load 'N' Go cargo tray with movable partitions. Meanwhile, the slide-out tailgate in Scion's Fuse concept goes one step further: It folds open to transform into a curb-high bench seat.

Photo courtesy of Faurecia

Photo courtesy of Jeep

Photo courtesy of Scion

Photo courtesy of Scion

Fold-Flat Seats

When the rear seats—and even the front passenger seat—fold flat, you wind up with a ton of usable cargo space, as you do here in the Dodge Hornet concept (left) and the Ford Fairlane concept. Check out the industrial-cool, durable materials chosen for the seatbacks, too: stainless steel in the Ford, honeycomb-texture rubber in the Mopar.

Photo courtesy of Dodge

Photo courtesy of Ford

35

36

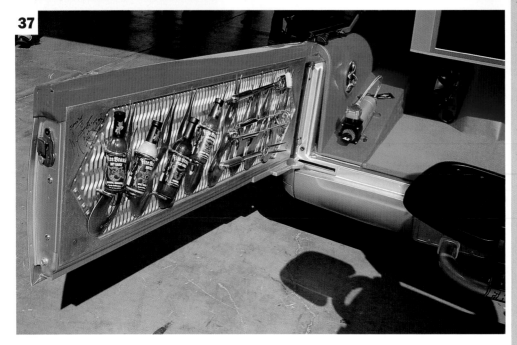

37

35 Going for something goth? How about a nice skull candelabra set off against black quilting? The fringe is just plain fun. This spider- and skull-bedecked 1923 Ford C-Cab is better known as the *Grim Reaper's Coach*.

36 Finish Line Automotive Interiors carried the door panel styling through to the rear of this 1937 Chevy, which sports an open interior with ample cargo-carrying space.

37 You know you're into tailgating when you plug a barbecue into your receiver hitch and turn your tailgate into one big sauce-and-grill tool rack. The flamed stainless-steel holders really make the look, don't you think? This 2005 GMC Canyon was built by Trent's Trick Upholstery.

Going to the Mat

Something as simple as a custom-fit mat can really jazz up a cargo area or a trunk and make it easier to keep clean. Intro-Tech Automotive's Sisal AutoMat (left) is woven from sisal (the fiber of the agave plant), while GG Bailey offers Car Couture carpet mats in patterns ranging from plaid and camo to styles reminiscent of Oriental carpets.

Photo courtesy of Intro-Tech Automotive   *Photo courtesy of GG Bailey*   *Photo courtesy of GG Bailey*

38 Sure, you could carry cargo. Or you could fill that back compartment with a roll cage, nitrous, and shocks, as Extreme Dimensions did in this race-ready Honda Fit.

1 Street Concepts managed the buildup of this incredible 1963 Cadillac DeVille for Kenwood. Gold Star Audio installed eight subwoofers where the back seat used to be and a KVT-910DVD head unit. Radi's Custom Upholstery made the rest of the interior look pretty, with lots of leopard-print detailing to match the outrageous paint. *Photo courtesy of Street Concepts*

Chapter 9
Audio and High-Tech Accessories

Want some crankin' road tunes? Movies and games to keep the kids entertained? A place to get some work done between sales calls?

When it comes to audio and high-tech accessories, you can go all-out in a show-stopping, eye-popping kind of way, or you can keep things subtle. You can fill up the trunk or the cargo area with amplifiers and speakers and subwoofers and

monitors and other gear. Or you can keep your storage areas usable and still install an incredibly high-fidelity—and incredibly loud—system that's practically invisible until you really start looking.

It's kind of like the difference between a tailored business suit and a sequined Grand Ole Opry get-up. It's simply a matter of style and personal taste.

2 Kicker speakers were nicely integrated into the doors and kick panels of this 1961 Chevy Impala. The enclosures were all painted gloss red to match the car's dash and body.

3 MIM Cars removed the center row of seats and built this custom limo-style divider for the Mercedes-Benz R550 named *Shot Caller*. The divider houses a 32-inch HD LCD monitor and a plethora of MTX Audio speakers and subs, pleasingly mounted in ascending size order.

4 Why not create your own drive-in theater? Five Axis fitted a giant screen under the hood of the Scion xA Speedster, along with a Casio XJ-560 projector. The concept car also sports two 19-inch Samsung monitors out back, three interlinked Xbox 360 gaming consoles, and a Pioneer HTP-2600 5.1 Dolby Digital surround-sound system. *Photo courtesy of Scion*

5 Holden's Efijy concept car features classic design cues from the iconic 1953 FJ Holden. Its modern, touch-control LCD screen even looks like a 1950s-era TV set. *Photo courtesy of Holden*

6 Alpine's 2003 Mini Cooper S won Best of Show for both People's Choice and Editor's Choice at the 2004 Consumer Electronics Show, and it remains a mind-blowing ride. The car no longer has doors; instead, the back portion—including the seat—slides out 5 feet. For maximum impact, two 12-inch Type X subwoofers port directly into the seatback. Alpine's Steve Brown and Mike Vu spent seven months and 4,000 hours on the buildup. *Photo by Carl Edwards, courtesy of Alpine Electronics*

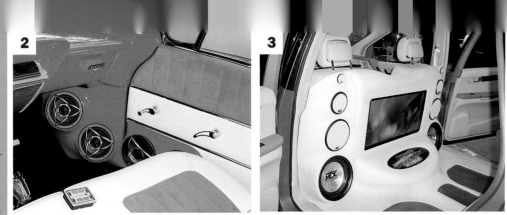

Mobile Office

Pretty much any vehicle can be turned into a mobile office these days—to varying degrees. From mild to wild: *Impression* (top left), a 1948 Chevrolet Blazer hot rod built by Pacific Coast Customs, has been outfitted with a computer, keyboard, and mouse. EDAG's *LUV* (Luxury Utility Vehicle, top right) started life as a Honda Ridgeline; it now features a pair of Intel-powered UltraMobile PCs mounted atop the front seats, so passengers in the rear can work, hold Web conferences, and, of course, play games. Meanwhile, the Becker/STRUT Escalade *ESV* is a full-on mobile conference room, with fore- and aft-facing seats, a sophisticated onboard computer system, broadband Internet connection, and printer/scanner capabilities.

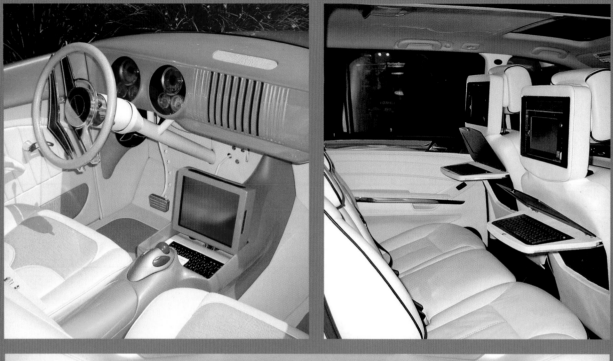

Photo courtesy of Becker Automotive Design

Trunks

7 This 1969 Camaro Z/28's trunk remains mostly stock and mostly usable, with a simple enclosure that makes the audio components and fire extinguisher equally accessible.

8 Just because you install a cool custom audio setup, that doesn't mean you can't carry a full-size spare and light it artfully, as in this JL Audio–equipped Shelby. *Photo courtesy of JL Audio*

9 We've come to expect monitors, DVD players, and big speakers in the trunk of late-model rides, but it's fun to see a 1949 Plymouth decked out for tailgating. It's the perfect setup for sitting behind your car all day at a car show, wouldn't you say? Soundsational handled the impressive installation.

10 Autocore installed not one but two flip-down 17-inch screens with built-in DVD players, along with two 7-inch monitors and two 12-inch subs in the trunk of *Dragzilla*, a Cadillac DeVille convertible. Love the finlets inside to match the big tailfins.

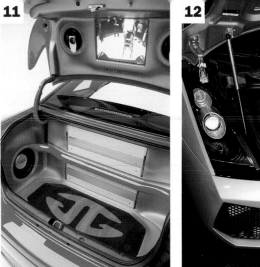

11 The still-very-usable trunk of this Pontiac GTO features Boston Acoustics Pro Series speakers, two GT amplifiers, and a 10-inch G2 subwoofer, along with a monitor on the inside of the deck lid. *Photo courtesy of Boston Acoustics*

12 Since it's a mid-engine machine, the audio components actually got tucked under the hood of this Lamborghini Murciélago. There could be enough room left for a couple small overnight bags, but you'd better pack light.

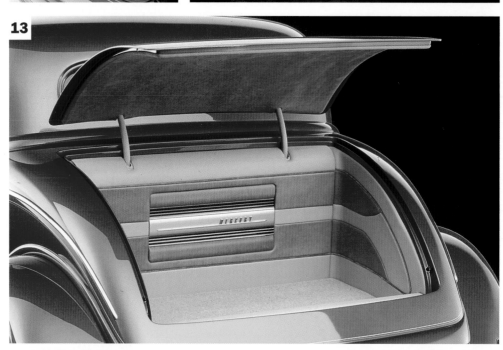

13 The trunk in *Stallion* looks as fresh as the day it debuted. The Chip Foose–built 1934 Mercury won the 2003 Ridler Award. Its understated trunk is a gorgeous example of audio integration, thanks to the work of Griffin Interiors. *Photo courtesy of Griffin Interiors*

14 Boston Acoustics' Chrysler 300 was outfitted with a two-channel GT amplifier and a pair of 12-inch G Series subwoofers in the trunk, each set behind a beautiful, backlit grille. *Photo courtesy of Boston Acoustics*

15 Good lighting can really set off an audio install, like this Rockford Fosgate–equipped 2006 Cadillac CTS-V built by Sound Xpression. *Photo courtesy of Rockford Fosgate*

16 Fesler flush-mounted audio components into all the surfaces within the trunk of this 1949 Mercury lead sled, built for Indianapolis 500 winner Buddy Rice. *Photo courtesy of Fesler Built*

17 ProRides built this stunning 1961 Ford Starliner, called *SR61*, for Summit Racing. The trunk showcases three MTX 1,500-watt amplifiers and two MTX 10-inch subs, with the fuel filler door visible through a window in the trunk floor. *Photo courtesy of Summit Racing*

18 A huge, suede-wrapped Mercedes emblem tops off the audio enclosure in this Benz. The Plexiglas provides a clear view into the Rockford Fosgate–filled area that used to be a back seat. *Photo courtesy of Rockford Fosgate*

19

20

21

22

19 Simple and clean. Fesler installed a pair of 10-inch Rockford Fosgate subwoofers and twin amps in the trunk of this 1969 Chevy Camaro. *Photo courtesy of Fesler Built*

20 Pepsi chose an Apple theme for its 2006 Mitsubishi Eclipse promo vehicle, which features a 20-inch iMac in the trunk. It's set up with a wireless Internet connection for surfing—while parked, of course. *Photo courtesy of Street Concepts*

Dashboards

21 Five Axis built the Fuse sports coupe concept for Scion. Passengers can watch movies, play video games, or do both, thanks to a pair of 10.5-inch monitors that span the dash. *Photo courtesy of Scion*

22 The factory Cadillac Escalade in-dash CD changer and navigation system now work with a Rockford Fosgate 3sixty.2 signal processor. This SUV is heavily modified, but changes to the dash are truly subtle: just the addition of three petite speakers. *Photo courtesy of Rockford Fosgate*

23 The interior design for the Kia Soul concept was inspired by high-end audio equipment, and the entire setup lets either the driver or front passenger play DJ. That notebook computer is mounted on a tray that swivels either way. *Photo courtesy of Kia*

Hidden Audio

Some audio installations are about highlighting every single piece of equipment, and some are more about hiding things away. The glove box is a traditional hiding place, as in this 1955 Chevy 210 with its hidden head unit, or this Rockford Fosgate–equipped Lexus, which sports a 3Sixty.2 signal processor and sound system gauges in the glove box, along with controls for the Tein adjustable shocks. Pickup trucks with fold-up rear seat bottoms provide a great hiding place for speakers and amplifiers, too.

Photo courtesy of Rockford Fosgate

Photo courtesy of Street Concepts

24

Behind the Seats

24 Yards of orange leather and subtle screens hide the premium Rockford Fosgate sound system inside the 1937 Ford better known as *Chocolate Thunder.* The car was built by Rad Rides by Troy. The Recovery Room handled the upholstery. *Photo courtesy of Rad Rides by Troy*

25 An assortment of speakers is discreetly hidden inside an enclosure behind the seats of this 1939 Ford Deluxe Coupe.

26 A Kenwood touchscreen head unit controls the almost completely hidden sound system inside the 1940 Ford called *Vision.* The system includes Rockford Fosgate's subwoofer, midrange and tweeter amplifiers, and a slew of speakers, like the ones hidden behind these sexy grilles. Rad Rides by Troy designed the car, and Griffin Interiors handled the inside jobs.

27 Ostrich adds some nice texture to the custom speaker enclosure inside the rear of a 2006 Scion tC. *Photo courtesy of CarSponsorships.com*

25

26

27

28 IcedOutEmz's Mercedes-Benz SL500 thumps nicely, thanks to a giant Kicker subwoofer built into the space behind the front seats.

29 Street Concepts built this 2003 Mitsubishi Eclipse, which is all painted and sueded inside. The back seat was replaced with three beautifully enclosed Kenwood dB+ subwoofers, thanks to Gold Star Audio. *Photo courtesy of Street Concepts*

30 A slew of Boston Acoustics products have taken up residence behind the seats of this 1973 Volkswagen Super Beetle, including Z Series speakers, six GT amplifiers, four 10-inch G5 subwoofers, and four 10-inch GTR TunableRadiators. That center bridge is lit with neon. *Photo courtesy of Boston Acoustics*

31 Once you have a roll cage, are you really going to put passengers in the back of your 1970 Plymouth Barracuda? Clearly not, if you've installed a pair of Kenwood subwoofers in a custom enclosure. Rad Rides by Troy built *Sick Fish* for *Fear Factor* TV show host Joe Rogan. *Photo courtesy of Rad Rides by Troy*

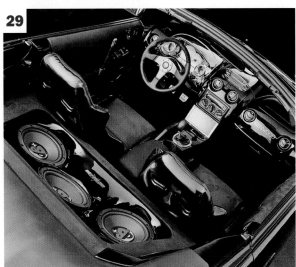

Seat Splitting

One way to keep back-seat passengers from getting too chummy, or getting any sleep, is to split the space between them with speakers—or, better yet, huge, protruding subwoofers—built into a nice leather-wrapped or painted enclosure. Cases in point, clockwise from top left: a beautiful 1957 Chevy Bel Air called *Black Mamba*, with leather work by Dan's Auto Upholstery; the 2004 Scion xA by L. J. Garcia with a full complement of Audiobahn speakers, subs, amps, and monitors and a Pioneer head unit (suede by Advanced Specialties); and a 1950 Mercury better known as *Mercules*, with state-of-the-art Pioneer equipment installed by Audio Art. This technique works between the front seats, too, as in the Sony Team Xplod Dodge Ram 2500 HD, with work by Audio Designs of Atlanta.

Photo courtesy of Scion

Looking Up

32 Here's a cool place to stash speakers: Fesler mounted a pair of Kickers up by the sun visors inside this 2006 Hummer H1 Alpha. *Photo courtesy of Fesler Built*

33 Sound Xpression built this 2006 Cadillac CTS-V that's packed with Rockford Fosgate gear, including a pair of speakers discreetly mounted in pillar pods on each A-pillar. *Photo courtesy of Rockford Fosgate*

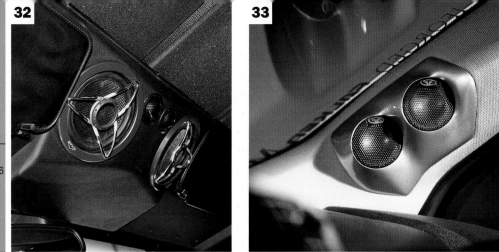

Head Units Overhead

A wide variety of off-the-shelf overhead consoles are designed to make mounting a head unit easy, freeing up space on the dash or center console. They can be painted or upholstered to match your ride, or you can opt for one of the finished metal models, which come polished or brushed. Or you can adopt this idea and craft your own unique design.

34

35

36

Cargo Areas

34 Five Axis transformed this Scion xB into a mobile DJ setup after getting input from numerous professional DJs about what they'd want in a dream-mobile. The slide-out area has a top rack with two traditional turntables and a bottom rack with two Pioneer CDJ-1000 digital turntables and a Pioneer DJM-600 mixer. Pioneer mid- and high-range speakers were mounted in the rear, while subwoofers fill the back part of the cabin. *Photo courtesy of Scion*

35 The *Wagonator*, a 1960 Chevy Brookwood station wagon, boasts seven monitors, including this Rosen Car Show Series unit out back, along with four Arc Audio Flat Line 12-inch subwoofers and four different Arc Audio amps. The amp rack was covered in Italian butterscotch leather to match the seats.

36 The Chrysler Town & Country Black Jack concept sports a slew of Azentek and Kicker components, including a 37-inch LCD flat screen out back flanked by Kicker speakers. *Photo courtesy of Mopar*

37 Stand next to this 1996 Chevy S-10 Blazer filled with Earthquake Sound equipment, and I'm quite sure you'll feel the earth move.

38 Clean, usable, and still really loud. This 2005 Mazda 6 wagon built by Street Concepts sports a Kicker amp sunk under the cargo area floor and a subwoofer set into a carpeted box, leaving actual room for cargo. Crazy. *Photo courtesy of Street Concepts*

39 Here's a cool camping setup: The Jeep Trailhawk concept features a pair of handsome, portable audio pods, each fitted with a dock for an MP3 player. It also has twin jerry can–style boxes done up in easy-to-spot Firewood Orange to hold first aid or road hazard gear. *Photo courtesy of Jeep*

40 Kicker amps, a Sony monitor, speakers, and subwoofers completely fill the small cargo space inside this C4 Corvette. The blue-flame paint pays subtle tribute to the original Corvette engine, plus it matches the car's wild exterior.

41

41 Believe it or not, that Rockford Fosgate Power T15kW unit provides an amazing *15,000* watts of power to *two dozen* speakers in this 2006 Cadillac Escalade ESV, which was built by the Rockford Technical Training Institute. *Photo courtesy of Rockford Fosgate*

42 This BMW proves that you can install a pretty hardcore audio system—complete with amps, tweeters, mid-range speakers, and subwoofers—and still have a totally usable cargo compartment. *Photo courtesy of Alpine Electronics*

43 How do you completely fill the back of a 2006 Chevrolet HHR? With a custom ported enclosure that's home to two hefty Alpine SWR-1542D 15-inch Dual 4-ohm subwoofers, each powered by an Alpine MRP-M850 mono sub amplifier. *Photo by Dana Maione, courtesy of Alpine Electronics*

44 Galpin Auto Sports' Navigator *LUX* looks luxurious, thanks to stunning Rau maple burlwood trim. Enclosures for the Arc Audio amps and Image Dynamic speakers have been painted to match the seats' Edelman Luxe Calf Cherry leather. *Photo courtesy of Galpin Auto Sports*

42

43

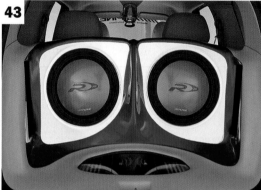

44

Speakers in the Doors

Speakers have been installed in door panels for as long as people have been improving the sound systems in their vehicles, and there are a zillion different ways to do it. Clockwise from top left: You can be subtle, as in this 1936 Plymouth, where holes in the shape of a speaker are the only giveaway. You can build one or more speakers into a custom armrest, as in this 1957 Chevy Cameo pickup. You can craft a whole or partial new door panel, as in this stunning suicide-door 1940 Ford, or as ProMotorsports did in this GMC Acadia. Or you can expand beyond speakers and integrate amps, too, as in this 1996 Chevy S-10 Blazer that's filled with Earthquake Sound equipment.

45

46

47

45 Fesler radically modified this now-topless 1969 Chevy Blazer, adding a huge Kicker sound system. A custom speaker enclosure replaced the rear seats, and what used to be the cargo area is now home to more speakers and a trio of amps. *Photo courtesy of Fesler Built*

46 D&P Classic Chevy's buildup of this 1965 Chevy Chevelle 300 appeared on the TV show *Chop, Cut, Rebuild.* The slammed two-door wagon sports gorgeous two-tone leather and major MA Audio subs along with a beautifully mounted monitor out back, and it still has room for luggage and humans, too.

47 Put this much JL Audio gear in the back of your SUV, and you can forget about using the rearview mirror. You'll need a rear-mount camera to see what's going on behind you. *Photo courtesy of JL Audio*

1 You don't have to be an artist to sketch some ideas as a jumping off point for discussions. On the other hand, you can *hire* an artist to do renderings of your interior—and to contribute ideas to the project. Heck, the renderings may even be suitable for framing later. This gorgeous illustration is the final seat design for Saturn's Flextreme concept. *Illustration courtesy of Saturn*

Chapter 10
From Ideas to Reality

Okay, now you've looked through the book. You've found a lot of ideas you'd like to emulate, or combine, or riff on, or improve.

So what's the next step? Well, that depends on what you want to do and how much you can do yourself.

Most of the hardware stuff is easy. If you can screw in a light bulb, you can change a shift knob. Changing the knobs on the dash is not much more difficult. Neither is replacing a rearview mirror. Most do-it-yourselfers can change

a steering wheel, as long as it's not air bag–equipped.

Certainly, you can add some cool-looking floor mats or a trunk or cargo area mat. Changing the carpet requires a bit more skill.

If you're pretty clever, you can probably craft some mounts to install late-model seats in a vintage ride. But upholstery is harder. Even if you order a kit that's been cut to fit your seats—such as a leather or suede upholstery kit from Katzkin—it still takes some skill to install it. Fortunately, there are plenty of upholstery shops, and it only takes a few inquiries at local car shows to find a shop that comes highly recommended.

Once you get beyond that, you enter the realm of custom fabrication—say, creating a custom console or a custom dashboard or molded door panels or an enclosure for audio components. Even creating a custom headliner is trickier than you might expect. In these cases, you'll need some real skills—or you may need some real help.

Fortunately, top interior shops across the country provide some of the same advice for would-be clients and for do-it-yourselfers. So I've gathered 10 tips to help you go from ideas to reality.

Tip No. 1: Collect Stuff for Show and Tell

If you plan to do the work yourself, how do you go from general ideas to an actual design? And if you're not going to be doing all the work yourself, how do you communicate your ideas to one or more people who will work on your car?

To start, take a hint from interior designers who work on homes, hotels, restaurants, and office buildings: They start with a three-ring binder. For a house, they often set up one section for each room, with all the ideas for that room grouped together. You can do the same. You can have one section for each aspect of your interior: one for the seats, one for the dash and gauges, one for the trunk or cargo area, and so on.

Within each of those sections, you can put together photos of what you like from this book, for example. Perhaps you love the shape of a particular armrest, but you like the brushed-metal finish on another one. Maybe you like the shape of a seat and the upholstery on a different one. You get the gist.

And don't be afraid to look well beyond the automotive world for inspiration. Some of the one-off seats in this book were inspired by home and office chairs. Some of the hardware was clearly inspired by plumbing supplies and bathroom fixtures. Some of the dashboards were inspired by vintage dressers and sideboards and other furniture. And many of the overall interior designs were inspired by aircraft or ships.

So gather together the ideas that you like, as random and disparate as they may at first appear. Because the whole purpose is to be able to express your aesthetic, which, as you've probably already discovered, is not always easy to put into words.

If you find swatches of material that you love, toss them in the binder, too. The same goes for paint chips. The more you can show, the less you have to tell.

Tip No. 2: Choose a Theme

Think about an overall theme for your vehicle. Do you want it to be nostalgic? Futuristic? Barebones? Hedonistic?

Do you want the ultimate in comfort? Some sort of a living room on wheels, complete with recliners and DVD players? Do you want a comfortable long-distance tourer? Or is comfort completely irrelevant?

Do you want a ride that's obviously modified in every way? Or do you like your modifications to be so subtle that people wonder what's stock and what's not?

Tip No. 3: Watch Out for Scope Creep

Modifying a vehicle's interior is surprisingly like remodeling a room at home. Scope creep becomes a factor.

Say you've got a relatively small budget and relatively modest desires. Maybe you just want to reupholster your vinyl seats in a nice, supple leather. Well, odds are, once you get the seats done, you're going to want the door panels to match. And then you may find that the carpet is the wrong color. And before you know it, you're installing a custom leather-wrapped console, wrapping the dash in leather to match, and installing a matching headliner.

In the end, you could wind up doing a complete interior redo, but without the planning and forethought that makes the job easier—and often less expensive—in the long run. Putting thought into the whole thing up front usually nets you better, more cohesive results, too.

So now's a good time to have a serious chat with yourself. Does some of this ring true? Are you the king or queen of scope creep? Will you be satisfied only by gutting the interior and starting from scratch?

Tip No. 4: Think About the Interior *Before* You Pick the Paint

The more you can figure out ahead of time, the better. For instance, if your dashboard originally came with a vinyl pad on top but you've decided to paint it body color, it's definitely better to have the exterior and the interior pieces painted at the same time. That's one surefire way to make sure they match.

Speaking of which, do you want your entire interior to match your exterior? It doesn't matter if you're going with a monochromatic look or something two-tone with pinstriping. It pays to think about the interior before you start work on the outside.

Why? For starters, there are far, far, far more colors of paint available on the market today than there are shades of leather or suede or even fabric. As Steve Pearson of Upholstery Unlimited says, "I have a car that we'll be doing fairly soon, and the owner wants to paint the car red. He actually got red leather samples from me first, and then he took those samples to select the paint color so he knew that it would match."

Tip No. 5: Pick and Choose What You'll Do

You certainly can build a spectacular, full-on custom interior yourself. Many of the cars and trucks in this book are home-built. The owner of the 1932 Ford called *Red Ram Special* actually taught himself how to do sheetmetal work so he could build his own interior panels and seats.

Of course, not everybody has the knack for such work—or the time to do it right.

Even if you've built the engine and done all the mechanical work on your car, there's no shame in letting the experts handle your car's interior. Heck, some of the biggest names in hot rod building—people like Chip Foose and Troy Trepanier—often outsource the interior work.

Now, you could choose to do *some* of the interior work yourself and then outsource the rest. Perhaps you might fit the seats and then have an upholstery shop cover them. Or maybe you'll have a metal fabrication shop build a custom dash and then you'll install the gauges. And of course it's really common to outsource the sound system installation; dialing in a mega-watt system is beyond the everyday know-how of a lot of folks.

Tip No. 6: Select a Shop

You can choose to work with different shops for different aspects of the interior. Or you could go all the way and have one shop do everything.

Having a single shop manage the whole interior build is sort of like having a general contractor in charge of your home remodel. One entity is ultimately responsible for making sure everything works—and for making sure everything works together.

Clearly, this arrangement reduces the likelihood of finger pointing, name calling, and the ever-popular blame game ("It's not *our* fault!") if things don't work out quite right. It also reduces the likelihood that you'll have to pay twice for the same work because, say, the kick panels that the audio shop built just don't work with the rest of the interior's aesthetic—or once everything is together, they just don't clear the doors or the dash.

Tip No. 7: Make Sure Your Aesthetics Are Similar

Obviously, you'll want to get references and referrals before you decide to work with a particular shop. But here's another point that's at least as important if you want to be truly happy with the results: Choose a shop with an aesthetic much like your own.

There's no point in going to a shop like Griffin Interiors, which builds interiors for clients like Foose Design and Rad Rides by Troy, if you want a super-futuristic look. Griffin doesn't do futuristic. It does clean and tailored and subtle.

So once you've got an overall design theme, make sure the shop you're planning to work with totally gets it and is happy to execute it.

Tip No. 8: Get Everyone on the Same Page

If you do decide to work with several shops—and be your own general contractor, so to speak—the wise move is to gather everyone together, literally. Sit down at the same time, in the same place, with representatives from each shop. If that's not logistically possible, set up a conference call or a Web conference. There are ways to make it work.

The goal is to make sure everybody understands what everybody else wants and needs. So, for instance, if the audio guys are building a custom speaker enclosure to replace the back seat, they have to know exactly where the roll cage is going to go. If a fab shop is building a custom dash, they have to know how much clearance the upholstery shop needs to wrap the dash in leather so it still fits perfectly inside the car.

Beside clearances and tolerances, there are other things to discuss. In many cases, the people at an audio shop will assume that you're going to run all the wiring under the carpet. But, as Pearson points out, carpet usually gets glued in, and that means the wiring will be inaccessible, or at least tough to access without making a big, old mess. So if you want to make sure the car is truly serviceable—as the top-notch builders do—then you want to get all the key players together as early in the process as possible.

Tip No. 9: Sketch It Out

You don't have to be an artist to draw some idea of what you want. Even some of the greatest automotive designers sometimes provide little more than a rough sketch to an interior shop. If nothing else, a drawing can be a jumping-off point for discussions of what you do and do not want.

And if you can't even begin to draw, you can always use tracing paper to copy the outline of a seat or a dashboard design that you like. Then you can make copies of that tracing and use those copies just like a coloring book, drawing in different colors and patterns between the lines to see what works best.

If you're computer hip, you can do the same sort of thing with PhotoShop or another photo-manipulation program, working with an actual image of a seat and then applying different colors, patterns, or textures. Or you can work with an actual photo of a dash and play with the placement or the design of different gauges, knobs, climate-control vents, monitors, and the like.

Tip No. 10: Make a Full-Size Mockup Before You Make Actual Components

And here's a real time-saving tip. You know how people always say, "Measure twice, cut once." This is even better advice from shops that have been there, done that many times: Cut a full-size mockup out of heavy paper or cardboard before you start building anything.

Your drawing may seem perfectly to scale, but it may be off just slightly. Well, just slightly on an 8x10-inch drawing can translate into a big gap in a full-size car.

What's more, what looks good on paper may require a little fine-tuning once you see it in the car. So make something you can play around with easily.

Then use your full-size mockup as a template when you're ready to work with wood, metal, fiberglass, or whatever materials you choose.

Jim Griffin from Griffin Interiors actually built an entire full-length console for *Corpala* (a 1963 Chevrolet Impala with Corvette underpinnings) from cardboard. Then he sent the cardboard mockup over to Eckert's Rod & Custom so the shop could build an actual console that would not only look great, but that would mate up perfectly with the dash and fit perfectly between the narrowed and reshaped factory bucket seats up front and the completely custom seats in back.

The more you can finalize a design before you start cutting, welding, and working with expensive materials, the better the finished product will be—and the more time, money, and aggravation you'll save.

Now go have some fun and craft a really creative interior!

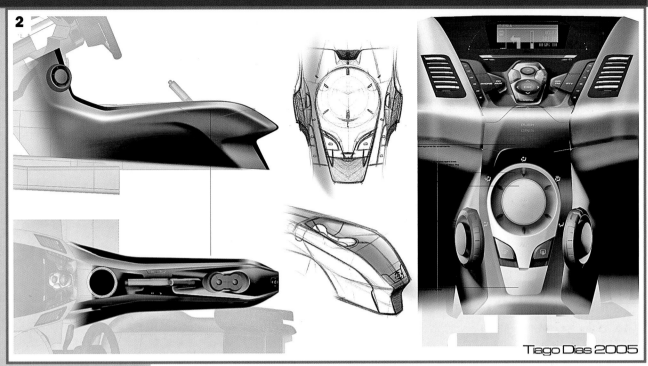

Tiago Dias 2005

2 Don't be afraid to play around with colors at the drawing stage. Can you imagine how different this dash/console design would have looked if it had been done in red or gold instead of blue—or with iridescent paint, metalflake, or pinstriping—or if the digital gauges had had blue or white readouts instead of red? *Illustration courtesy of Ford*

3 Chip Foose may create beautiful, frame-worthy illustrations for all of the interiors on the TV show *Overhaulin'*, but he can provide pretty rough sketches to Griffin Interiors for actual vehicle buildups, such as this 1940 Cadillac resto rod called *Miss Vivy*. *Illustration courtesy of Griffin Interiors*

4 Here's how *Miss Vivy*'s actual interior turned out. It's amazing how much information can be conveyed with just a few strokes of a pen or pencil. *Photo courtesy of Griffin Interiors*

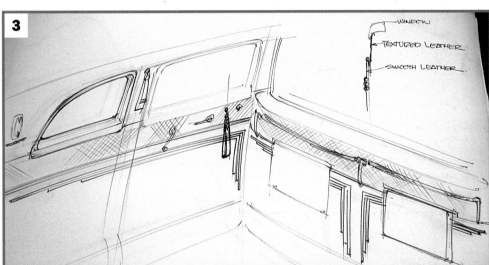

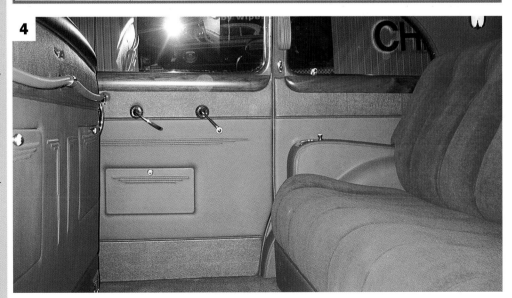

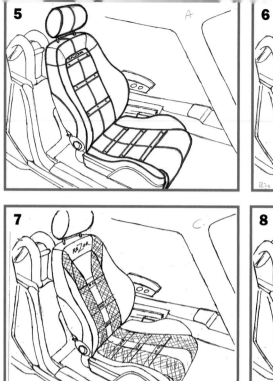

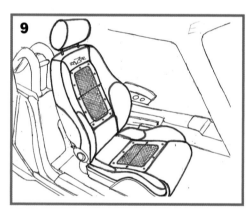

5–9 Even after you've chosen a seat, there are plenty more choices to make. Upholstery Unlimited provided Ringbrothers and the car owner with several different stitch pattern and trim design ideas for the 1969 Chevrolet Camaro called *Razor. Illustrations courtesy of Upholstery Unlimited*

10 The final Camaro seat design was pretty close to one of the illustrations. This car won Goodguys' Street Machine of the Year award in 2008. *Photo courtesy of Upholstery Unlimited*

11 The more full-size mockups you can do before you start cutting and fabricating, the better the finished product will be—and the less time and materials you'll waste. Here, Fesler tries out an instrument panel design in a 1966 Ford Mustang. *Photo courtesy of Fesler Built*

12, 13 Griffin Interiors made a highly detailed console out of cardboard so Eckert's could craft an actual piece that would fit perfectly in this 1963 Chevy Impala. The full-length console is wrapped in leather, and it extends from under the dash to between the rear seats.

Resources

AC Schnitzer
www.ac-schnitzer.de/en

Adams Rod & Custom
Penticton, BC
250-492-7637

Advanced Specialties
La Habra, CA
562-694-5650
www.advancedspecialties.com

Air Ride Technologies
Jasper, IN
812-481-4787
www.ridetech.com

All Ways Hot Rods
Phoenix, AZ
602-442-5199

Alpine Electronics
Torrance, CA
800-ALPINE-1 (800-257-4631)
www.alpine-usa.com

America's Most Beautiful
  Roadster Award
Grand National Roadster Show
Rancho Cucamonga, CA
877- ROD-SHOW
www.hotrodshows.com

Appleman Interiors
Lancaster, OH
740-756-4295

Arc Audio
Modesto, CA
866-258-0288
www.arcaudio.com

Armand's Auto Upholstery
Walnut Creek, CA
925-934-4373

Audio Designs of Atlanta
www.audiodesignsof
  atlanta.com

AutoCore Kustoms
Phoenix, AZ
602-216-2673
www.autocorekustoms.com

Auto Meter
Sycamore, IL
866-248-6356
www.autometer.com

AutoTrader.com
888-512-0094
www.autotrader.com

B&M Racing & Performance
  Products
Chatsworth, CA
818-882-6422
www.bmracing.com

Becker Automotive Design
Oxnard, CA
805-487-5227
www.beckerautodesign.com

Big Al's Carponents
San Bernardino, CA
877-712-1027
www.bigalscarponents.com

Billet Specialties
La Grange, IL
708-588-0505
www.billetspecialties.com

Blastolene
www.blastolene.com

Divine's Custom Creations
Pittsburg, CA
925-252-9585
www.divinescustomcreations.com

Bonspeed
Anaheim, CA
714-666-1999
www.bonspeed.com

Boston Acoustics
Peabody, MA
978-538-5198
www.bostonacoustics.com

Boyd Coddington's Pro's Pick
See Goodguys Rod & Custom As-
  sociation

Brothers
Corona, CA
800-977-2767
www.brotherstrucks.com

Budnik Wheels
Huntington Beach, CA
714-892-1932
www.budnik.com

California Custom & Classics
Fontana, CA
909-829-8500

Caresto
Ängelholm, Sweden
www.caresto.se

Carlsson Autotechnik
www.carlsson.de

CarSponsorships.com

Casio
www.casio.com

CEC (Claus Ettensberger
  Corporation)
Gardena, CA
310-767-1111
www.cecwheels.com

Chop Cut Rebuild
www.ccr.tv

Cimtex Rods
Jarrell, TX
512-746-2707
www.cimtexrods.com

Classic Design Concepts
Novi, MI
866-624-7997
www.classicdesign
  concepts.com
www.cdcflashback.com

Classic Instruments
Boyne City, MI
231-582-0461
www.classicinstruments.com

Consumer Electronics
  Show (CES)
www.cesweb.org

D.A.D. Mercedes
Garson
Los Angeles, CA
310-533-1647
www.garson-usa.com

Dakota Digital
Sioux Falls, SD
605-332-6513
www.dakotadigital.com

Dan's Upholstery & Auto Trim
Lake Tomahawk, WI
715-277-4247
www.dansupholstery
  autotrim.com

Detroit Street Rods
Carolina Beach, NC
910-458-3838
www.detroitstreetrods.com

D&P Classic Chevy
Huntington Beach, CA
714-375-0889
www.dpchevy.com

Dominator Street Rods
Brentwood, CA
925-625-9235
www.dominatorusa.com

Downtown Willy
Torrance, CA
www.downtownwilly.com

DUB Magazine
www.dubmag.net

DuPont Hot Hues
Houston, TX
www.dupont.com

Earthquake Sound
Hayward, CA
510-732-1000
www.earthquakesound.com

East Bay Muscle Cars
Brentwood, CA
925-516-CARS (2277)
www.eastbaymusclecars.com

Eckert's Rod & Custom
Molalla, OR
503-263-2893
www.eckertsrodand
    custom.com

EDAG
www.edag.de

Eddie Salcido
See Hi-Speed Rods & Customs

Eddie's Rod & Custom
Cedar Rapids, IA
319-393-1937

Edelman Leather
(to the trade only)
New Milford, CT
800-866-TEDY
www.edelmanleather.com

Edog Designs
951-788-4941 or 714-469-1512
www.edogdesigns.com

Enviro Textiles
Glenwood Springs, CO
970-945-5986
www.envirotextile.com

Extreme Dimensions
Fullerton, CA
888-611-AERO
www.extremedimensions.com

EZ Boy Interiors
Indian Orchard, MA
800-423-6053
www.ezboyinteriors.com

FastLane Rod Shop
Donahue, IA
563-843-2067
www.fastlanerodshop.com

Faurecia
www.faurecia.com

Fesler Built
Phoenix, AZ
602-953-8944
www.feslerbuilt.com

FiftySixDelux
www.fiftysixdelux.com

**Finish Line Automotive
    Interiors**
Santa Clara, CA
408-919-0000
www.finishlineinteriors.net

Five Axis
Huntington Beach, CA
714-842-9677
www.fiveaxis.net

Foose Design
Huntington Beach, CA
www.chipfoose.com

**Gabe's Street Rods
    Custom Interiors**
San Bernardino, CA
909-884-5150
www.gabescustom.com

**Gaffoglio Family
    Metalcrafters**
Fountain Valley, CA
714-444-2000
www.metalcrafters.com

Galpin Auto Sports
Van Nuys, CA
877-GO-GAS-GO (464-2746)
www.galpinautosports.com

Galvin Precision Machining
Santa Rosa, CA
707-526-5359
www.galvinprecision.com

GG Bailey
Calhoun, GA
866-6-GG-BAILEY
    (866-644-2245)
www.ggbailey.com

Glide Engineering
Rancho Cucamonga, CA
800-301-3334
www.glideeng.com

Gold Star Audio
Irvine, CA
949-752-1446
www.goldstaraudio.com

**Goodguys Rod & Custom
    Association**
Pleasanton, CA
925-838-9876
www.good-guys.com

Gore-Tex
www.gore-tex.com

Grant Products
Glendale, CA
818-247-2910
www.grantproducts.com

Griffin Interiors
Bend, OR
541-389-8612
www.griffininteriors.us

Haneline Products
Morongo Valley, CA
888-878-8678
www.haneline.com

Hi-Speed Rods & Customs
Tucson, AZ
www.hispeedcustoms.com

HiTek Hot Rods
Dayton, OH
937-277-9488
www.hitekhotrods.com

Hollywood Hot Rods
Burbank, CA
818-842-6900
www.hollywoodhotrods.com

Hot Rides by Dean
Moorpark, CA
888-865-DEAN (3326)
www.hotridesbydean.com

The Hot Rod Company
Deerfield, WI
608-217-5689
www.thehotrodcompany.com

IcedOutEmz
702-362-ICED (4233)
www.icedoutemz.com

Image Dynamics
www.imagedynamicsusa.com

Intro-Tech Automotive
Chino, CA
714-635-3007
www.intro-techautomotive.com

JL Audio
www.jlaudio.com

JME Enterprises
Jamul, CA
619-669-9904
www.jmeenterprises.com

John D'Agostino Kustom Kars of
California
Discovery Bay, CA
www.johndagostino
kustomkars.com

Jon Lind Interiors
Eugene, OR
541-465-1233

JS Custom Interior
Salt Lake City, UT
801-597-6493

Juliano's Hot Rod Parts
Ellington, CT
800-300-1932
www.julianos.com

Katzkin Leather Interiors
Montebello, CA
323-725-1243
www.katzkin.com

Kaucher Kustoms
Santa Monica, CA
310-656-9993
www.kaucherdesignwerks.com

Kenwood USA
Long Beach, CA
800-KENWOOD (536-9663)
www.kenwoodusa.com

Kicker
Stillwater, OK
405-624-8510
www.kicker.com

Kindig-It Design
Salt Lake City, UT
801-262-3098
www.kindigit.com

Kool Rides
koolrides.hosting-
advantage.com

Livin' the Low Life
www.bciitv.com

Lokar Performance Products
Knoxville, TN
877-469-7440
www.lokar.com

Lux Interiors
Phoenix, AZ
480-980-5080
www.luxinteriorsaz.com

MA Audio
Rancho Dominguez, CA
310-223-0400
www.maaudio.com

Mark III Customs
Ocala, FL
866-836-2823
www.markiiicustoms.com

Max's Upholstery
Riverside, CA
951-352-0601

Meguiar's
Irvine, CA 92614
800-347-5700
www.meguiars.com

Metalcrafters
Monmouth, IL
309-734-3511
www.metalcraftersonline.com

MIM Cars (Marketing In
Motion)
Lake Forest, CA
949-204-7258
www.marketinginmotion
online.com

Mini Motoring Graphics
www.minimotoringgraphics.com

Mitch Henderson Designs
McKinney, TX
www.mitchhenderson
designs.com

Monster Garage
www.monstergarage.com

Mothers Polishes Waxes
Cleaners
Huntington Beach, CA
714-891-3364
www.mothers.com

MTX Audio
Phoenix, AZ
800-225-5689
www.mtx.com

Nordskog Instruments
Anaheim, CA
714-991-9999
www.nordskogperformance.net

Original Wraps
Lakewood, CO
720-746-1600
www.originalwraps.com

OZE Rod Shop
St. Benoit, Quebec
418-227-3144
www.ozerodshop.net

Pacific Coast Customs
American Canyon, CA
707-224-4011
www.pacificcoastcustoms.com

Painless Performance
Products
Ft. Worth, TX
817-244-6212
www.painlessperformance.com

Panoz Auto Development
Company
Hoschton, GA
888-GO-PANOZ (467-2660)
www.panozauto.com

Pioneer
www.pioneerelectronics.com

Plasticolor
Fullerton, CA
800-367-2087
www.plasticolorinc.com

Popular Hot Rodding
www.popularhotrodding.com

POSIES
Hummelstown, PA
717-566-3340
www.posiesrodsand
    customs.com

PPG Automotive Refinish
Strongsville, OH
440-572-2800
www.ppgrefinish.com

Precision Coachworks
Billerica, MA
800-322-1940
www.precisioncoachworks.com

ProMotorsports
417-848-2210
www.promotorsportspower.com

ProRides
Warrendale, PA
724-940-3322
www.goprorides.com

Pyramid Street Rods
Bellingham, WA
www.lockitsocket.com

Quality Metalcraft (QMC)
Livonia, MI
734-261-6700
www.qualitymetalcraft.com

Radi's Custom Upholstery
Garden Grove, CA
714-534-2915

Rad Rides by Troy
Manteno, IL
815-468-2590
www.radrides.com

Rage Imports
Whitfield Racing Inc.
Upland, CA
877-472-4300
www.rageimports.com

Rawlings
www.rawlings.com

Recovery Room
Plattsmouth, NE
402-235-3800
www.recoveryroomrod
    interiors.com

Rick Dore Kustoms
Phoenix, AZ
602-547-3512
www.rickdore.com

Ridler Award
Detroit Autorama
www.autorama.com

Ringbrothers
Spring Green, WI
608-588-7399
www.ringbrothers.com

Rockford Fosgate
www.rockfordfosgate.com

**Ron Mangus Custom Hot Rod
    Interiors**
Rialto, CA
909-877-9342
www.customautointeriors.com

Rosen Entertainment Systems
Corona, CA
951-898-9808
www.rosenentertainment.com

Roush Performance
Livonia, MI
800-59-ROUSH
www.roushperformance.com
Russ' Trim Shop
Harrisburg, PA
717-564-5084

Samsung
www.samsung.com

Santana Interior Designs
www.santanainteriors.com

Scott's Hotrods 'n Customs
Oxnard, CA
805-485-0382
www.scottshotrods.com

**SEMA (Specialty Equipment
    Market Association)**
Diamond Bar, CA
909-396-0289
www.sema.org

Shadowrods
989-754-1927
www.shadowrods.com

Skoty Chops Kustoms
San Carlos, CA
www.myspace.com/skoty
    chopskustoms

Sony Electronics
San Diego, CA
858-942-2722
www.sony.com/xplod

Sound Choice Audio
Grand Island, NY
716-775-3333
www.scapusa.com

Soundsational
Eugene, OR
866-470-2523
www.soundsational.com

Sound Xpression
Phoenix, AZ
602-438-0352
www.soundxpression.com

Spectre Performance
Ontario, CA
909-673-9800
www.spectreperformance.com

Spinneybeck Leather
Getzville, NY
800-482-7777
www.spinneybeck.com

Stewart Warner
Lancaster, PA
866-797-7223
www.stewartwarner.com

Stoked Out Specialties
Rockwall, TX
972-772-0146
www.stokedoutspecialties.com

Street & Performance
Mena, AR
479-394-5711
www.hotrodlane.cc

Street Concepts
Anaheim, CA
714-630-3030
www.streetconcepts1.com

Summit Racing
Tallmadge, OH
800-230-3030
www.summitracing.com

Sunpro
Cleveland, OH
800-228-7667
www.sunpro.com

Sun Spec Billet Factory
Osage Beach, MO
800-927-6921
www.ssbilletfactory.com

Tein USA
Downey, CA
562-861-9161
www.tein.com

**Three Crowns Speed
& Kustoms**
Reno, NV
775-355-RODS
www.threecrownsreno.com

T.J. Pagano
www.pinheadlounge.com/
pagano

Trent's Trick Upholstery
Baltimore, OH
740-468-2727
www.trentstrickupholstery.com

Upholstery Unlimited
Clinton, IA
563-242-7607
www.wecoveritall.biz

Jimmy Vasser Chevrolet
www.jimmyvasser
chevrolet.com

**VDO Performance
Instruments**
www.sso-usa.com/performance

Vintage Air
San Antonio, TX
800-TO-COOL-U (862-6658)
www.vintageair.com

West Coast Customs
Corona, CA
951-284-0680
www.westcoastcustoms.com

Wild Rod Factory
St Jean de la Lande, QC
418-657-2963
www.wildrodfactory.com

Wise Guys Seats
Elkhart, IN
866-494-7348
www.wiseguys-seats.com

Wrocket Products
Foresthill, CA
530-367-2984

Zero Halliburton
www.zerohalliburton.com

Index